Published in the United States in 1999 by
Contemporary Books
A division of NTC/Contemporary Publishing
Group, Inc.
4255 West Touhy Avenue
Lincolnwood (Chicago), Illinois 60646-1975 U.S.A.

ISBN 0-0892-2666-9

**Commissioning Editor** Suzannah Gough
**Managing Editor** Kate Bell
**Editorial Assistant** Tanya Robinson
**Copy Editor** Norma MacMillan

**Art Director** Leslie Harrington
**Art Editor** Alison Fenton
**Stylist** Wei Tang
**Food for Photography** Meg Jansz
**Typesetting** Olivia Norton

**Picture Research** Rachel Davies
**Production** Amanda Sneddon

Cataloging-in-Publication Data is available from the
United States Library of Congress
Printed and bound in China by Toppan

**Page 1** *Sticky Rice with Peanuts (page 37)*
**Pages 2–3** *Green Mango Salad (page 99)*
**Pages 4–5** *Hot and Sour Fish Soup (page 18)*

*café*

# vietnam

**Annabel Jackson**

**Photography by Jeremy Hopley**

CONTEMPORARY BOOKS

# Contents

# Introduction

In Vietnam, you can see the doctor, the dentist, or the barber on the street. You can have a manicure or a pedicure, get a broken zipper mended, or give blood. Hardly surprising, then, that you can also eat on the street, and eat extremely well. Up and down the country, restaurants—in the traditional sense—hardly dare emulate the specialties of the street. For the food on the street is the real food of the country, the food that the Vietnamese have traditionally eaten since they were children and which they steadfastly continue to eat today.

Whether a traditional bowl of noodles (*pho*), a banana-leaf parcel of sticky rice (*xoi*), fresh spring rolls (*goi cuon*), or fresh stuffed rice cakes (*banh cuon*), the very best of the street dishes is usually found in the particular city or town of origin. And in every town and city there is always a woman who specializes in just that dish, one woman who cooks it better than any other. If she does not serve it literally on the street or at a table in the market, she will have set up a makeshift corner restaurant (probably in her house) and will be selling her special dish from there. A stall or store front is not even necessary. One young woman in Hue crouches near the sidewalk just outside her house, in front of a heavy-based pan on a charcoal grill in which she makes banana fritters, selling them to passersby as she flicks the sweet-smelling pieces hot from the pan.

The enjoyment of street food is not subject to age or gender. Elegant young women sit with perfectly straight backs on tiny chairs, eating a miniature dish of sweet rice-flour balls; young men gather in friendly groups for a beer and a plate of chicken's feet; fathers hop off their bicycles to buy corn-on-the-cob and chunks of sweet potato cooked on streetside charcoal grills for the children. During the parched summer months, everyone stops for two minutes to drink a glass of freshly squashed sugar-cane juice, its heady natural sweetness spiked with a squeeze of kumquat.

The invigorating experience of Vietnamese food culture does not begin when the chopsticks sink into a chicken broth rich with ginger and star anise, or when a spoon slides into crème caramel (a dessert so widely available that the Vietnamese have probably forgotten it was originally introduced by the French). It really starts with watching the preparation of food, which can be astonishing: the chopping of vegetables into tiny pieces, the steaming of batter into a translucent wrapper, the folding of a banana leaf. And all these tasks are performed at speed and with consummate skill. Even with experience, it can take hours to prepare just one dish. At home, a cook will allow almost one hour per dish, and that may well not include the cooking time. Often a dish

can be anticipated even before your arrival at the food stall. The delicious smell of pork patties browning over a charcoal grill alerts you that there is a *bun cha* stall nearby. The sound of batter hitting a sizzling pan announces that someone is making stuffed pancake, *banh khoai*, famous for the crispiness of its shell.

Street eating is so common in Vietnam that no one bats an eyelid at the more contemporary forms the custom is now taking. Over an espresso at a trendy coffee terrace in central Hanoi, a customer makes a sign to the shoeshine boy sitting outside, who rushes off to buy a bowl of beef noodles. Balancing the bowl on a tray, he delivers it to the table, complete with lime wedges and chili sauce.

Food culture is everywhere to be seen, even beyond the little street stalls with their tiny, colored plastic stools, wooden benches, and low tables, or among the women who might start preparations at 4 a.m. to have breakfast ready for the passersby. There is no need to go to a fancy restaurant to eat real Vietnamese food—just visit the market.

Every district has its own market, which housewives visit twice daily to buy fresh fish and meat, herbs and vegetables, some of them introduced by the colonial French and grown in the cooler climes around the city of Dalat. Stall-holders sell shredded fresh lemon grass, chopped fresh red chilies, and flaked crab meat. Coconuts, both young green ones and the older brown ones, are stacked high. There are green papayas, which never go out of season. Close by are stalls selling bottles of *nuoc mam*, the fermented fish sauce that defines the flavors of Vietnamese food. Another stall sells sheets of fresh vermicelli and rice noodles or egg noodles in various shapes and sizes. One stall is given over to rice papers, and the next to dozens of different kinds of rice.

In the areas between the markets, vendors sell fruit and vegetables from bamboo baskets, walking the streets with their perishables or crouching on the sidewalk where demand is high. The housewife pops around the corner for a little bag of freshly roasted peanuts or a pack of tamarind pulp for the sour soup she is creating. On a rainy evening in Hue, a vendor wanders up and down residential lanes calling out that he has baguettes for sale; the baguettes are piled high on his bicycle, covered with black plastic to keep off the rain. Another man is selling steamed dumplings from a cabinet on the back of his bicycle.

In this collection of recipes, the richness of Vietnamese street food is brought to the Western kitchen. Once the garlic and shallots are sizzling in the pan, the fresh green herbs are chopped to release their perfumes, the aromatic stocks are gently bubbling, and the lemon-grass-marinated pork is spitting happily on the grill, the cook can begin to get an exciting sense of what Vietnamese food—and Vietnamese life—is all about.

# The Vietnamese pantry

**Asian eggplant** (ca tim)  *Light purple in color, these are long and thin (8 inches long and no more than 2 inches diameter). There is no need to salt them first to remove excess liquid, and they cook quickly and easily.*

**Chilies** (ot)  *Like the Thais, the Vietnamese use tiny, very hot, fresh red chilies for cooking, for marinades, sliced or minced for sprinkling over food, and as a condiment. Larger red chilies are less hot and more often appear as decoration.*

**Vietnamese chili sauce** (tuong ot)  *is thick and either smooth or contains the seeds, and it is reddish-orange in color. Chili paste is a thicker version of chili sauce.*

**Cinnamon** (dinh huong)  *Cinnamon bark is harvested in Vietnam, and is readily available in chunky, 12-inch-long pieces. Freshly ground cinnamon is also used. Most "cinnamon" sold in Europe and North America is actually cassia, which is the bark of a type of laurel tree; although stronger than true cinnamon, it can be substituted.*

**Coconut** (dua)  *Vietnamese cooks use the coconut in many ways: as juice (found in the young green coconut), as white flesh (from the hard brown coconut), and as milk (made by soaking the grated flesh in water).*

**Canned coconut milk**  *is an excellent subsitute for freshly made.*

**Garlic** (toi)  *An essential flavoring in Vietnamese cooking, often used raw in dipping sauces such as* nuoc cham.

**Ginger** (gung)  *Although not as common a flavoring as in other Southeast Asian cuisines, the Vietnamese use ginger in dishes like* pho bo *and* pho ga. *Ginger is also steeped with fresh green tea leaves to make a delicious drink.*

**Herbs**  *In Vietnam, herbs grow in abundance, and a plate of fresh herb leaves appears on the table as commonly as salt, pepper, and* nuoc mam. *Many Vietnamese herbs, such as* ngo gai *(saw-leaf herb) and* rau ram, *which has no English name, are hard to find outside Southeast Asia. Fresh cilantro, mint, Italian basil, and Thai basil make a good compromise. Add Japanese* shiso *(also called perilla and Japanese basil) if you can find it. An herb platter should also include lettuce and mustard greens, beansprouts, seeded cucumber slices, and, if available, thinly sliced green (unripe) banana and star fruit.*

**Lemon grass** (xa)  *The stalks of this plant impart a unique spicy lemon fragrance and flavor. Fresh lemon grass is preferable to dried lemon grass, although the latter is acceptable (soak it before*

*use). Remove the tough outer leaves, and use only the tender core. The quantities given in this book are based on stalks about 10 inches long.*

**Lime** (chanh)  *Vietnamese salads almost always contain lime juice, and it is often mixed with salt and pepper to make a dipping sauce. Nuoc cham, which is the equivalent of soy sauce on the Chinese or Japanese table, is made from lime juice, water, sugar,* nuoc mam *(fish sauce), chilies, and garlic.*

**Aromatic lime leaves** (la chanh), *which come from a different tree (the Southeast Asian makrut tree), are used like bay leaves to flavor soups and curries.*

**Mushrooms**  *Dried Chinese mushrooms, light or dark brown in color, are used in many dishes, particularly meat stuffings. Grown on straw from paddy fields, straw mushrooms (nam rom), which are at least 1 inch high, are also very popular. Rarely available fresh in the West, they can easily be found canned.*

**Noodles**

**Cellophane noodles**  (bun tau) *are made from green mung beans. These very fine noodles are used, chopped, in meat fillings for items like spring rolls, or soaked and presented cooked on the herb platter (see left) for filling rice-paper or green-leaf rolls.*

**Egg noodles** (mi) *are similar to Chinese egg noodles. Dried or fresh and yellow in color, they are used in stir-fries and soupy noodle dishes.*

**Rice noodles** *Fine, almost translucent rice noodles are made from white rice flour; some are colored yellow with turmeric. In Vietnam, rice noodles, in various shapes and sizes, are available fresh at the market each morning—very fine vermicelli* (banh hoi), *flat noodles* (hu tieu), *thin noodles* (bun), *and large round noodles* (mi). *Dried rice sticks* (pho) *and dried vermicelli are excellent substitutes.*

**Nuoc mam** *This thin, brown sauce, made from fermented salted anchovies, is the definer of Vietnamese cuisine, being added to almost everything as a seasoning. The best sauces, rich in protein, are pungent in both taste and odor. If you can't find* nuoc mam, *use an anchovy-based fermented fish sauce such as* nam pla, *but increase the amount.*

**Peanuts** (dau phong) *Lightly roasted and crushed peanuts are sprinkled on salads and other dishes. You can roast freshly shelled peanuts quickly in a frying pan over high heat.*

**Rice** *Both long- and short-grain rice are eaten. Glutinous rice* (nep), *with short grains that cook into a sticky mass, is used for the breakfast dish,* xoi, *and for traditional dishes at* Tet (Lunar New Year). *The black version has a nutty flavor, and keeps its shape well. A flour ground from glutinous rice is used for making sweet dumpling desserts.*

**Rice flour** *is also used to make rice papers* (banh trang), *the very thin, semi-transparent rounds used to wrap up all manner of delicious mixtures, such as for spring rolls. Rice papers are usually available dried, and must be moistened to soften them before use.*

**Rice vinegar** *Fermented rice yields rice vinegar* (dam), *delicate in flavor, which is used in dipping sauces and salads as an alternative to the sourness of lime juice or tamarind pulp.*

**Scallions** (hanh) *Always minced, the white bulb and leafy green top are used separately. The white portion is generally stir-fried as a base for many dishes, and the green is tossed onto dishes just before serving.*

**Sesame seeds** (me) *White sesame seeds are frequently included in dishes such as salads for added texture.*

**Shallots** (hanh) *These sweet, mild members of the onion family are sliced or chopped and then sautéed to provide the base for many dishes. Fine slices of shallot are also deep-fried until crisp and sprinkled on top of dishes. Prepared this way and well drained, they can be kept in an airtight jar for a few weeks.*

**Soy sauce** (nuoc tuong) *Use a light, mild, Japanese soy sauce rather than a dark, strong, Chinese one in Vietnamese dishes.*

**Star anise** (bat giac) *This fragrant star-shaped spice has a flavor reminiscent of aniseed or licorice. It is used in five-spice powder and is an important flavor in one of Vietnam's most traditional dishes, the noodle soup* pho.

**Tamarind** (me) *The dry brown pods of this tree are harvested in Vietnam, but few people start from scratch, preferring to buy the pulp, which is readily available in blocks in the West. The sour, bright flavor of tamarind is important in Vietnamese soups, in particular.*

**Yellow beans** (dau xanh), *mung beans with the green shell removed, are widely used, in stuffings and sauces and as toppings. Soak the dried beans overnight or for at least 6 hours before use.*

Ingredients illustrated on previous pages
**Top row** (*from left to right*) *cinnamon sticks; cellophane noodles; soy sauce; coconut milk and fresh coconut; chili sauce and chilies; lemon grass, limes, and lime leaves.*
**Middle row** (*from left to right*) *Italian basil and Thai basil; Asian eggplants; fresh and roasted peanuts; nuoc mam; mint and cilantro; dried mushrooms and straw mushrooms.*
**Bottom row** (*from left to right*) *long-grain rice, rice vinegar, glutinous rice, black rice, and rice papers; sesame seeds and star anise; shallots and scallions; egg noodles; tamarind pods; garlic and fresh ginger.*

# The Vietnamese kitchen

The typical Vietnamese family kitchen—in both country and urban areas—is small, simple, and quietly organized. There is often very little food stored beyond *nuoc mam* (fish sauce), cooking oil, and a few condiments such as salt, sugar, and pepper. Daily—or more often twice-daily—visits are made to the market for the freshest of everything, from green leafy vegetables and seafood, to spices that are ground as you wait and bags of hot, freshly roasted peanuts.

The washing of baskets of green leafy vegetables and herbs is one of the most time-consuming activities in the Vietnamese kitchen. Often lit with just a single bulb and ventilated through a crack in the ceiling or an open window, the kitchen may not have running water, so much of the preparation work is done outside in the yard, or at a table in another room.

Brightly colored plastic mesh bowls, in all sizes, are used to hold the washed herbs and vegetables and, turned upside down, to protect fresh food. There are mesh ladles and tiny little mesh baskets for blanching noodles and beansprouts, bamboo or metal skewers, wooden chopsticks, little metal soup spoons, and teaspoons with long handles.

For cutting there are small, sharp vegetable knives and lethal-looking choppers hefty enough to take the top off a coconut. There are also special knives, rather like potato peelers, which are used for chopping lemon grass, and a little wood wedge with metal rings at one end designed for cutting green papaya into slivers. Vietnamese cooks are highly skilled at rapidly reducing vegetables or hard fruits to fine, if irregular, julienne strips.

A wooden mortar and pestle is traditionally used for grinding together flavoring ingredients such as shallots, garlic, lemon grass, and chili. However, more modern households have a food processor for such time-consuming tasks, as well as for mincing meat or fish.

Most kitchens feature a pair of electric burners, a tea kettle, and, most important, a free-standing charcoal (or wood-fired) grill. The grill is often used for simmering and steaming as well as for grilling meat and vegetables. For street cooking and at market stalls, such grills are the only means of cooking available. Cooking over charcoal imbues many dishes with a unique flavor.

The Vietnamese use a wok—smaller in both diameter and depth than the typical Chinese wok—for sautéeing, deep-frying, and occasional stir-frying. But more frequently they employ metal pans that have two small handles and a lid, which is removed with chopsticks or a cloth. These pans range in size from 6 inches diameter and 3 inches deep, to one large enough to make stock for a dozen bowls of noodles. Not every family has a steamer, so a plate on a little stand or metal mesh tray, set inside a wok or pan, is often used. For very quick steaming, food is simply placed in a covered pan over low heat, where it produces enough of its own liquid—and thus steam—to cook through.

Every kitchen has a range of claypots, always shallow, but ranging in width from 2 inches up. Roughly thrown but with surprisingly well-fitting lids, these rustic, richly colored pots are used for cooking all kinds of meat, fish, rice, and vegetable dishes.

Rolling and wrapping are key techniques in Vietnamese cuisine. There are many different ways to cut or fold the leaves or rice papers, but the most essential rule is that the wrapping should be neither tight nor loose. Rolling at the table is a far more casual affair, though, as the idea is to create a roll that can be easily bitten into.

**Right** *Shrimp and Pork Rolls (page 36)*

# BORDERS
## BOOKS AND MUSIC

4575 ROSEWOOD DR
PLEASANTON CA 94588
(925) 227-1412

STORE: 0117   REG: 01/06   TRAN#: 0526
SALE          05/19/2001   EMP: 00101

CAFE VIETNAM
        6468923     IR T          2.99

              Subtotal           2.99
              CALIFORNIA 8.00%     .24
1  Item       Total              3.23
              CASH               5.23
              CASH               2.00-

        05/19/2001 11:33AM

  THANK YOU FOR SHOPPING AT BORDERS
PLEASE ASK ABOUT OUR SPECIAL EVENTS

Visit our website at www.borders.com!

# APPETIZERS

# Crab and Asparagus Soup

Sup Mang Tay Cua

*This dish, served in restaurants and cafés all over the country, clearly shows the French influence on Vietnamese cooking—it was the French who introduced asparagus to Vietnam. Asparagus grown in the temperate climate of Dalat is now readily available in markets, particularly in the south—as is ready-flaked fresh crab meat.* **Serves 4–6**

**1 quart chicken stock**

**4 dried Chinese mushrooms** *soaked in warm water for 30 minutes, then thinly sliced*

**8 ounces (about 2 cups) crab meat** *flaked*

**1 tablespoon cornstarch** *mixed with a little cold water*

**1 egg** *beaten*

**6 asparagus spears** *thinly sliced diagonally*

**sea salt and freshly ground black pepper**

**8 quail eggs** *hard-boiled*

**chopped cilantro for garnish**

**1** Bring the stock to a boil. Add the mushrooms and crab and simmer for about 30 minutes, or until the mushrooms are soft.

**2** Gradually stir the cornstarch mixture into the soup, followed by the beaten egg. Add the asparagus and season to taste with salt and pepper. Cook gently for about 3 minutes.

**3** Serve hot, topping each portion with 2 quail eggs, some chopped cilantro, and freshly ground black pepper.

# Hot and Sour Fish Soup

Canh Chua Ca

*The Vietnamese would use a whole fish in the stock for this soup, particularly the head which has such sweet flesh, but use fish fillets if you prefer. Fish such as perch, pike, sea bass, and garoupa, or grouper, are suitable; the soup can also be made with raw tiger prawns, cooking them in the broth intact and then peeling them to eat.* **Serves 4–6**

**10-ounce whole fish or fish fillets**

**1 teaspoon sea salt**

**1½ cups okra sliced diagonally**

**8 ounces tomatoes** *each cut into eight wedges*

**½ cup beansprouts**

**1 fresh hot red chili** *thinly sliced*

**2 teaspoons tamarind pulp**

**1 tablespoon *nuoc mam***

**½ cup peeled fresh pineapple cut into small segments**

**1 tablespoon minced fresh *rau om* (if available)**

**1** If using a whole fish, cut it into three. Place the fish or fillets in 3½ cups boiling water, add the salt, and simmer for about 10 minutes, or until the fish is soft. Remove the fish with a slotted spoon.

**2** Add the okra, tomatoes, beansprouts, and chili to the fish stock. Simmer for about 10 more minutes, or until the vegetables are tender.

**3** Meanwhile, soften the tamarind pulp in a few tablespoons of the fish stock in a small pan over low heat. Remove the seeds, then add the resulting tamarind paste to the soup.

**4** Add the *nuoc mam* and the fish and simmer for a further 5 minutes.

**5** Add the pineapple and *rau om*, if using, and simmer for another 5 minutes. Check the seasoning and serve.

# Chicken and Lotus Seed Soup

Ga Tan Hat Sen

*Lotus seeds used to be so expensive that only the Emperor could afford to eat them. Today they are within most people's budgets, but this dish still retains its regal connections and is traditionally served at weddings. The Vietnamese buy fresh lotus seeds in season and use dried seeds for the rest of the year. Canned seeds can also be used; just drain them and add to the soup at step 4.* **Serves 6**

**1** Simmer the lotus seeds in their soaking water for about 1 hour, or until they are almost soft.

**2** Meanwhile, mix the chicken with the shallots and ½ teaspoon each salt and pepper. Leave to rest for 30 minutes to allow the flavors to blend.

**3** Heat a wok or pan, add a little oil, and heat it, then flash-fry the chicken mixture, stirring constantly, for about 2 minutes, or until the strips of chicken are white and opaque.

**4** Put the stock in a saucepan and bring to a boil. Add the chicken mixture, drained lotus seeds, and mushrooms. Simmer for 15–20 minutes or until the lotus seeds are soft to the touch.

**5** Sprinkle the scallions and freshly ground black pepper on the top of the soup and serve.

**1 ounce dried lotus seeds** *soaked in warm water for 1 hour*

**12 ounces boneless chicken breast** *chopped into small strips (about 2 cups)*

**10 shallots** *minced*

**sea salt and freshly ground black pepper**

**vegetable oil for frying**

**7½ cups chicken stock**

**1 ounce dried Chinese mushrooms** *soaked in warm water for 30 minutes, then thinly sliced*

To finish:

**6 scallions** *minced*

# Sizzling Stuffed Pancake

Banh Xeo

*Xeo refers to the sizzling sound made as the batter for the very thin pancake (banh) hits the hot oil. A smaller version of this dish, from the former Imperial capital, Hue, is called banh khoai, which translates literally as "happy cake." The ingredients for the filling may seem to lack excitement, but the dish is as much about textures as about flavors. The crêpe-like pancakes should be as thin as possible so as to be very crisp.* **Makes about 6 pancakes**

**1** Cook the yellow beans in boiling water until soft but still firm. Drain and set aside.

**2** Combine the batter ingredients in a bowl. Add 1½ cups water and stir until smooth.

**3** Heat a little vegetable oil in an 8-inch frying pan. Sauté the shrimp, onion, and pork over medium heat for about 2 minutes, stirring frequently. Transfer to a bowl and add the yellow beans and beansprouts.

**4** Lightly oil the frying pan and heat over high heat, then pour in about ½ cup of the batter. Quickly swirl the batter around the pan to cover the bottom thinly and evenly. Almost immediately tip out the excess batter, pouring it back into the batter remaining in the bowl.

**5** Pile a layer of filling on one half of the pancake, then fold the other half over. Cover the pan and cook for about 5 minutes, or until the pancake is crisp.

**6** To eat, break each pancake into pieces and roll inside leaves with a selection of herbs, cucumber slices, and green banana and star fruit slices.

For the filling:

**⅓ cup dried yellow beans** *soaked overnight*

**vegetable oil for frying**

**4 ounces peeled cooked small shrimp**

**½ onion** *chopped*

**4 ounces boneless pork loin** *thinly sliced (about 1 cup)*

**1 cup beansprouts** *blanched briefly to soften slightly*

For the pancake batter:

**2 cups rice flour**

**½ teaspoon each ground cumin and sea salt**

To serve:

**leaves of mustard greens and/or lettuce**

**sprigs of fresh herbs such as basil, Thai basil, cilantro and mint**

**English cucumber** *seeded and thinly sliced*

**green (unripe) banana and green (unripe) star fruit** *thinly sliced*

# Hue Rice Rolls in Banana Leaf
Banh La

*Hue chef Nuoc Tinh would probably not approve of these rolls being made in aluminum foil, but the recipe does work this way if you cannot get hold of banana leaves. Light and delicate, this dish is typical of regal Hue cooking.* **Makes about 30 rolls**

**30 pieces of banana leaf (each 8 x 4 inches)** *softened and cleaned in boiling water* **(or use aluminum foil)**

For the rice cakes:

**1 cup rice flour**

**1 teaspoon vegetable oil**

For the filling:

**8 ounces peeled cooked small shrimp**

**1 teaspoon vegetable oil**

**1 tablespoon minced scallions**

**½ teaspoon *nuoc mam***

**pinch of sugar**

**sea salt and freshly ground black pepper**

For the *nuoc cham* dipping sauce:

**1 tablespoon *nuoc mam***

**3 tablespoons lime juice**

**1 garlic clove** *minced*

**1 fresh hot red chili** *minced*

**½ teaspoon sugar**

**1** Combine the rice flour and 2½ cups water in a saucepan and beat with a wooden spoon over low heat until thick and smooth. Remove from the heat and cool. Stir in the oil.

**2** To make the filling, pound the shrimp almost to a powder in a mortar and pestle or smash them using a fork. Heat the oil in a shallow pan and cook the scallions for about 1 minute, squashing them as you stir. Add the shrimp and continue to cook and squash the mixture for about 5 minutes until it is quite dry. Add the *nuoc mam*, sugar, a pinch of salt, and ½ teaspoon pepper.

**3** Spread a scant teaspoon of the rice-flour mixture onto the center of each piece of banana leaf (to make an oblong about 1½ x 5 inches). Sprinkle a scant teaspoon of the shrimp mixture along the center of the rice oblong. Fold the long edges of the leaf over the top, pressing firmly but carefully, and then fold the short edges under, to end up with a parcel about 1½ x 5 inches. Flatten the parcel gently, ensuring that the filling is evenly distributed. Steam for 5–10 minutes, or until the rice cake is translucent.

**4** Meanwhile, combine all the ingredients for the dipping sauce with 2 tablespoons water.

**5** Remove each rice cake from its wrapper and gently roll up the rice cake. Serve warm, dipped into *nuoc cham*.

# Steamed Rice-Paper Rolls

Banh Cuon

*An exciting culinary sight on the streets of Vietnam is that of a woman skillfully making a paper-thin rice-flour pancake on a piece of cheesecloth stretched over a pot of steaming water. The process takes about 20 seconds and involves a single chopstick. The procedure in this recipe is rather more simple.* **Makes 10–15 rolls**

**1** To make the rice-paper pancakes, combine all the ingredients in a food processor with 2 cups water. Whiz until smooth. Leave the batter to rest in the refrigerator for 1 hour. Meanwhile, mix the pork with the *nuoc mam*, ¼ teaspoon each salt and pepper, and half the garlic. Leave in a cool place for 1 hour, so the flavors can blend.

**2** Heat a little oil in a frying pan and sauté the onion, shallot, and remaining garlic until soft. Add the pork mixture and cook until beginning to brown. Add the turnip and thinly sliced mushrooms and cook for a further 5 minutes. Keep the filling warm.

**3** Lightly oil and heat an 8-inch nonstick frying pan. Beat the batter, then pour about 2 tablespoons into the pan, swirling to distribute it evenly. Cover and steam the pancake for 2–3 minutes, or until translucent and firm. Toss out of the pan and let rest for 1–2 minutes before filling.

**4** To make each roll, place about 2 teaspoons of the pork filling in a band along the center of a pancake, roll up, and then chop into two or three pieces. Alternatively, place the same amount of filling in the center of a pancake, fold in the sides, and then roll up from bottom to top.

**5** Serve warm, wrapped with beansprouts and herbs inside green leaves, and dip into *nuoc cham*. Alternatively, place a few pieces in a bowl along with herbs and beansprouts, and spoon *nuoc cham* on top.

For the rice-paper pancakes:

**½ cup rice flour**

**¼ cup each potato flour and cornstarch**

**¼ teaspoon sea salt**

**2 tablespoons vegetable oil, plus extra for frying**

For the filling:

**½ cup ground pork**

**½ teaspoon *nuoc mam***

**sea salt and freshly ground pepper**

**1 garlic clove** *minced*

**½ onion** *minced*

**1 shallot** *minced*

**1 cup finely chopped Asian turnip (or use ordinary turnip)**

**5 dried Chinese mushrooms** *soaked in warm water for 30 minutes*

To serve:

**beansprouts**

**sprigs of fresh herbs such as basil, cilantro, and mint**

**leaves of mustard greens and/or lettuce**

**nuoc cham dipping sauce (see page 22)**

# Prawn Mousse on Sugar Cane

Chao Tom

*It is vital to use fresh sugar cane as it imparts a special flavor to the prawn mousse. The Vietnamese would pound the prawns with a mortar and pestle, but a food processor makes the job much easier.* **Makes 12 sticks**

**12 sticks ripe sugar cane** *each peeled and cut to a 4-inch length*

For the mousse:

**1 pound raw tiger prawns or jumbo shrimp** *peeled and deveined*

**2 tablespoons ground pork fatback**

**1 tablespoon minced shallots**

**1 garlic clove** *minced*

**1 teaspoon cornstarch**

**½ teaspoon each sugar, sea salt, and freshly ground black pepper**

**1 egg white**

**vegetable oil for greasing**

To serve:

**leaves of mustard greens and/or lettuce**

**sprigs of fresh herbs such as basil, Thai basil, cilantro, and mint**

**nuoc cham dipping sauce (see page 22)**

**1** For the mousse, combine the prawns, pork fatback, shallots, garlic, cornstarch, sugar, salt, and pepper. Leave to rest in the refrigerator for about 1 hour.

**2** Place the prawn mixture in a food processor and whiz until smooth. Stir in the egg white.

**3** Grease your hand with a little vegetable oil. For each stick, place about 2 tablespoons of the prawn purée in your palm and gently wrap it around the middle of a stick of sugar cane, pressing it on lightly. Cover the exposed ends of the stick with foil.

**4** Grill over a medium charcoal fire, or cook under a preheated broiler, for about 5 minutes, turning to cook evenly. Remove the foil.

**5** To serve, eat the mousse straight off the cane, or cut the mousse off the cane into pieces and serve wrapped in green leaves with herbs, dipped into *nuoc cham.*

# Grilled Pork Patties

Nem Nuong

*The aroma of this specialty from Nha Trang, in the center of Vietnam, is a real appetite-stimulant. Rice powder, which can be made in quantity and kept, serves to bind and flavor the ingredients. The patties are normally wrapped with green leaves inside fresh rice papers (some street stalls even add a rolled-up deep-fried rice paper), but a simpler lettuce-and-herb wrapping is just as delicious.* **Makes about 12 patties**

½ cup glutinous rice

8 ounces (1 cup) ground lean pork

2 tablespoons ground pork fatback

1 shallot *minced*

1 garlic clove *minced*

1 tablespoon *nuoc mam*

sea salt and freshly ground black pepper

vegetable oil for greasing

To serve:

leaves of mustard greens and/or lettuce

English cucumber *seeded and thinly sliced*

scallions *shredded*

green (unripe) banana and green (unripe) mango *thinly sliced*

sprigs of fresh herbs such as basil, Thai basil, cilantro, and mint

*nuoc cham* dipping sauce (see page 22)

**1** To prepare the rice powder, soak the glutinous rice in warm water for about 1 hour. Drain and dry, then throw into a hot heavy-based pan. Stir over low heat for about 15 minutes or until the rice is golden in color. Reduce to a fine powder in a coffee grinder or food processor. These quantities make more than you will need for this recipe, but the roasted rice powder will keep in an airtight jar for up to 3 months.

**2** Mix the pork with the pork fatback, shallot, garlic, and *nuoc mam*. Season with a pinch each of salt and pepper and bind with 1 tablespoon roasted rice powder. Leave to rest in the refrigerator for 30 minutes.

**3** Grease your palms with a little oil, then form the pork mixture into small patties or sausage shapes. Grill over a medium charcoal fire, or cook under a preheated broiler, for about 15 minutes, turning from time to time, until golden brown.

**4** Serve wrapped in green leaves with the cucumber, scallions, green banana and mango, and the herbs, and dip into *nuoc cham*.

# Pan-Fried Eel Patties

Cha Luon

*Ask your fish merchant to remove the skin and the bones from the eel for you.*
**Makes about 12 patties**

**1** Combine the eel, white fish, shallots, lemon grass, *nuoc mam*, sugar, salt, and pepper, mixing well. Cover and leave for about 30 minutes in the refrigerator, to allow the flavors to blend.

**2** Form into small, round patties about 2 inches in diameter. Gently fry in butter for about 5 minutes, or until golden brown on both sides.

**3** To eat, wrap with sprigs of herbs in green leaves and/or rice papers and dip into *nuoc cham*.

**1 pound eel** *ground*

**8 ounces white fish fillet** *ground*

**4 shallots** *minced*

**2 stalks fresh lemon grass** *minced*

**1 teaspoon *nuoc mam***

**½ teaspoon each sugar, sea salt, and freshly ground black pepper**

**butter for frying**

To serve:

**leaves of mustard greens and/ or lettuce and/or rice papers**

**sprigs of fresh herbs such as basil, Thai basil, cilantro, and mint**

***nuoc cham* dipping sauce (see page 22)**

# Spring Rolls
Cha Gio

*Vietnamese spring rolls are more delicate than the Chinese version, and there are many variations in ingredients, shape, and size in different parts of the country. This recipe balances fish and meat with vegetables, giving the filling an excellent texture.*

**Makes 24 rolls**

**12 dried rice papers (8 inches in diameter)**

**1 egg white**

**vegetable oil for deep-frying**

For the filling:

**½ cup ground pork**

**½ cup flaked crab meat**

**¼ cup minced peeled raw shrimp**

**¼ cup finely chopped taro root**

**2 tablespoons finely chopped Asian turnip (or use ordinary turnip)**

**½ ounce dried Chinese mushrooms** *soaked in warm water for 30 minutes, then minced*

**½ ounce cellophane noodles** *softened in warm water, then chopped*

**pinch each of sea salt and freshly ground black pepper**

To serve:

**sprigs of fresh herbs such as basil, Thai basil, cilantro, and mint**

**leaves of mustard greens and/or lettuce**

***nuoc cham* dipping sauce (see page 22)**

**1** Combine the filling ingredients, mixing well.

**2** Soften each rice paper by lightly brushing it with warm water on both sides and leaving it for 20 seconds. Using scissors, cut each paper in half. Then, with the straight edge at the bottom, place a generous teaspoon of filling in the center of each rice-paper half. Wrap the sides over, then roll up tightly from the bottom, squashing the filling into all corners. Use a little egg white to seal the roll, if necessary.

**3** Deep-fry the rolls until golden brown. Serve wrapped with herbs inside green leaves, dipping in *nuoc cham* before eating.

# Vegetable Spring Rolls

Choi Gio Chay

*A great Asian vegetarian dish, this does not, like so many, pretend to be meat in either texture or appearance. The recipe is based on one created by award-winning chef Quach Thien Tuong, from Ho Chi Minh City.* **Makes 20 rolls**

**10 dried rice papers (8 inches in diameter)**

**1 egg white**

**vegetable oil for deep-frying**

For the filling:

**⅓ cup dried mung beans** *soaked overnight*

**2 ounces firm beancurd (tofu)** *chopped*

**1 cup finely chopped taro root**

**½ ounce dried Chinese mushrooms** *soaked in warm water for 30 minutes, then minced*

**pinch of sugar**

**sea salt and freshly ground black pepper**

To serve:

**sprigs of fresh herbs such as basil, Thai basil, cilantro, and mint**

**English cucumber** *seeded and thinly sliced*

**green (unripe) banana and green (unripe) star fruit** *thinly sliced*

**leaves of mustard greens and/ or lettuce**

***nuoc cham* dipping sauce (see page 22)**

**1** Cook the mung beans in fresh water to cover for about 20 minutes or until soft. Drain. Combine the mung beans, beancurd, taro, and mushrooms. Add the sugar and ½ teaspoon each salt and pepper and mix together well.

**2** Soften each rice paper by brushing lightly with warm water on both sides and leaving for about 20 seconds. Using scissors, cut each paper in half. Then, with the straight edge of the paper at the bottom, place a generous teaspoon of filling at the center of each rice-paper half. Wrap the sides over, then roll up tightly from the bottom, squashing the filling into all corners. Use a little egg white to seal the roll, if necessary.

**3** Deep-fry the rolls until golden brown on all sides. Serve wrapped with sprigs of herbs and slices of cucumber, and green banana and starfruit inside green leaves, dipping in *nuoc cham* before eating.

# Cabbage and Carrot Rolls

Bap Cai Don

*This recipe comes from a young woman named Tuyen who lives in Hue, and who is reputed to be one of the best home cooks in the city. The secret of the dish's success is to remove all excess liquid so that the rolls will be firm.* **Makes about 12 rolls**

**1** Blanch the cabbage leaves for about 1 minute, then drain and pat dry. Remove any tough stems.

**2** Sprinkle the carrots with 1 tablespoon salt, and stir and toss thoroughly. Set aside for about 10 minutes. Rinse the carrots and drain well, pressing out any excess liquid. Add the sugar, lime juice, garlic, and a pinch of salt and toss to mix.

**3** Place a cylinder of the carrot mixture toward the bottom of each cabbage leaf. Roll up tightly from the bottom into a roll about 1 inch in diameter. Remove any ragged ends, then cut the roll across into pieces about 2 inches long.

**4** To serve, garnish with sprigs of mint (the leaves can be eaten with the rolls). Eat plain or dipped into *nuoc cham*.

**4–5 large Chinese or Napa cabbage leaves**

**1 pound carrots** *finely grated*

**sea salt**

**1 tablespoon sugar**

**juice of 1 lime**

**1 small garlic clove** *minced*

To serve:

**sprigs of fresh mint**

**nuoc cham dipping sauce (see page 22)**

# Sautéed Clams with Toasted Sesame Rice Crackers

Ngheu Xue Banh Trang

*Unlike so many Vietnamese dishes, this is extremely quick to make. It is a great pre-dinner snack or could be served to accompany other dishes during a meal.* **Serves 2–4**

**1** If using untoasted crackers, broil or lightly bake until they are crisp and beginning to brown. Leave to cool.

**2** Heat a little oil in a small, heavy-based frying pan and sauté the garlic for about 1 minute. Add the clams and sauté, stirring, for 2 minutes. Add the sugar, half of the chopped herbs, ½ teaspoon salt, and a little pepper. Cook for a further 1 minute, stirring constantly.

**3** Sprinkle the clams with the remaining herbs and the sesame seeds. If using larger crackers, break them into pieces. Eat the clams from the crackers or cracker pieces.

**2–4 sesame rice crackers (8 inches in diameter) or a package of small ones**

**vegetable oil for frying**

**2 garlic cloves** *minced*

**8 ounces (about 1 cup) fresh shucked clams**

**1 teaspoon sugar**

**2 tablespoons minced fresh *rau ram* (or use Thai basil)**

**sea salt and freshly ground black pepper**

**2 teaspoons white sesame seeds**

# Shrimp and Pork Rolls

Goi Cuon

*One of the most delightful and popular dishes in Vietnamese cuisine, these rolls are quite different from anything else in Southeast Asian cooking. They are deliciously light and healthy. Leftover roast pork can be readily utilized.* **Makes 8 rolls**

**8 dried rice papers (8 inches in diameter)**

**1 head lettuce**

**½ cup beansprouts** *ends removed*

**a selection of fresh basil, mint, and cilantro leaves**

**4 ounces rice vermicelli** *boiled quickly in water*

**4 ounces boneless pork** *boiled and thinly sliced (about 1 cup)*

**16 medium shrimp** *steamed and peeled*

***nuoc cham* dipping sauce (see page 22)**

**1** Soften the rice papers by lightly brushing each one with warm water. Then, after about 20 seconds, fold in about 1 inch on the two opposite sides and the top.

**2** For each roll, place a leaf of lettuce on a rice paper and pile on a few beansprouts, herb leaves, and vermicelli. Add some pork and 2 shrimp, and roll up.

**3** Serve the rolls immediately, with the *nuoc cham* for dipping.

# Sticky Rice with Peanuts

Xoi

*Neither sweet nor savory, but an explosion of different tastes, this is a traditional breakfast dish normally eaten from a little banana-leaf packet. It is very heavy and very filling. There are many different colors and flavorings; this version is cooked by a street vendor in Nha Trang, who gets up at 4 a.m. to begin preparing it, ready for the breakfast crowd.*

**Serves 4–6**

**1** Steam the rice with the blanched peanuts for about 30 minutes or until it is suitably soft and sticky but not mushy.

**2** Meanwhile, cook the yellow beans in boiling water for 15–20 minutes, then drain and mash.

**3** Serve the rice and peanut mixture on small plates, dividing the toppings among the servings.

**1 heaping cup glutinous rice** *soaked overnight*

**1 cup shelled peanuts** *blanched*

For the toppings:

**3 tablespoons dried yellow beans** *soaked overnight*

**4 shallots** *thinly sliced and deep-fried until crisp*

**2 teaspoons each sugar and sea salt**

**2 tablespoons sesame seeds** *lightly toasted*

**3 tablespoons slivers of fresh coconut** *lightly toasted*

# Grilled Beef in La Lot Leaves

## Bo La Lot

*La lot, or piper leaves, have a distinctive half-vegetal, half-spicy quality. They are not always easy to find outside Vietnam; however, grape leaves, which are similar in shape and size, make an excellent substitute. The stuffed rolls are served with* nuoc cham, *which is the equivalent of soy sauce on the Chinese or Japanese table—rarely does one see a Vietnamese meal without some variety of this dipping sauce.* **Makes 15 rolls**

15 *la lot* **leaves (or use grape leaves)**

**vegetable oil for brushing**

For the filling:

**8 ounces (1 cup) ground beef**

**¼ cup ground pork fatback**

**2 teaspoons five-spice powder**

**1 teaspoon each ground cinnamon and turmeric**

**2 stalks fresh lemon grass** *minced*

**1 garlic clove** *minced*

**1 teaspoon each sugar, sea salt, and freshly ground black pepper**

To serve:

**leaves of mustard greens and/or lettuce**

**sprigs of fresh herbs such as basil, Thai basil, cilantro, and mint**

*nuoc cham* **dipping sauce (see page 22)**

**1** Wash the *la lot* leaves. (If using grape leaves packed in brine, soak well in hot water to remove all salt.) Pat dry.

**2** Mix together the filling ingredients and leave to rest in the refrigerator for at least 1 hour.

**3** Using a generous teaspoon of filling per roll, place the meat mixture in the center of the leaf. Fold over the sides of the leaf first, then roll up tightly from the bottom. Brush the rolls with oil and grill over a medium charcoal fire, or cook under a preheated broiler, for about 10 minutes, turning to cook evenly.

**4** To eat, wrap a beef roll in a green leaf with a selection of herb leaves, and dip in the *nuoc cham*.

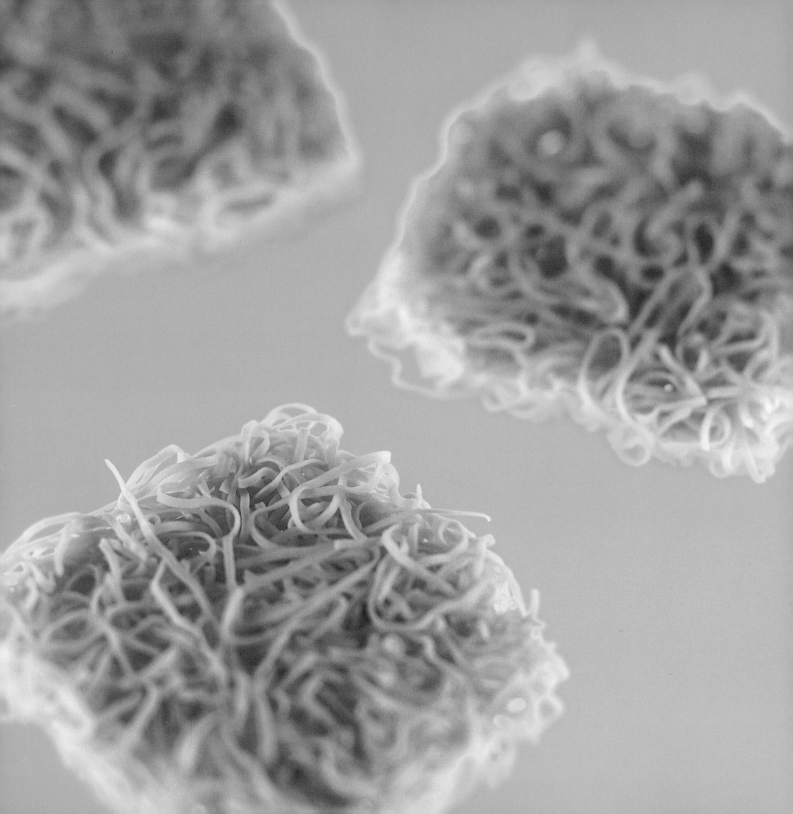

# MAIN
## DISHES

# Grilled Fish in Banana Leaf
## Ca Nuong La Chuoi

*Banana leaf does little to enhance the flavor of the fish here, though as it burns it serves to chargrill the shallots and chilies in the marinade. Banana leaf is, of course, more exotic than aluminum foil, which nonetheless is a good alternative.* **Serves 4**

**1-pound whole fish or 4 fish fillets (4 ounces each)**

**bunch of banana leaves** *softened and cleaned in boiling water* **(or use aluminum foil)**

For the marinade:

**8 shallots** *thinly sliced*

**2 fresh hot red chilies** *thinly sliced*

**4 stalks fresh lemon grass** *minced*

**4 garlic cloves** *minced*

**4 teaspoons each *nuoc mam* and vegetable oil**

**4 teaspoons each sugar, sea salt, and freshly ground black pepper**

**1** Combine the marinade ingredients in a dish. Add the fish and turn to coat, then leave to marinate in the refrigerator for at least 30 minutes.

**2** If using banana leaves, tear fine strips off one leaf to make strings for tying up the parcels.

**3** Wrap the fish in 2–3 layers of banana leaf, spooning the marinade onto both sides, and tie securely with banana-leaf strings. (Alternatively, wrap the fish in individual pieces of aluminum foil.)

**4** Grill over a medium charcoal fire, or cook under a preheated broiler, for about 20 minutes, turning to cook evenly. Open up the parcels and serve in the leaves, or discard the charred leaves before serving, if preferred.

# Grilled Fish with Lemon Grass and Chili

Ca Nuong Xa Ot

*This recipe works well with all kinds of fish fillets or whole fish, in particular tuna, pike, and garoupa (grouper).* **Serves 4**

**4 fish fillets or 1 whole fish**

**vegetable oil for basting**

For the topping:

**2 tablespoons minced fresh lemon grass**

**4 fresh hot red chilies** *minced*

**2 garlic cloves** *minced*

**1 tablespoon vegetable oil**

**2 teaspoons sea salt**

**½ teaspoon each sugar and turmeric**

**1** Mix together the ingredients for the topping.

**2** Oil a baking pan and lay the fish on it (if using fillets, put them close together). Spread the topping over the fish. Cook under a preheated broiler, about 5 inches from the heat, for about 20 minutes or until the fish is cooked. Baste with oil regularly to prevent the topping from drying out.

# Hanoi-Style Fried Fish

Cha Ca Hanoi

*This legendary dish is so well loved that Cha Ca La Vong, the most famous restaurant in Hanoi serving it, even had a street named after it. Very traditional Vietnamese cooks use ca lang fish marinated in a mixture of the juice from fresh turmeric and galangal bulbs, the juice of a potent fermented shrimp paste, and a fermented rice juice. This recipe, which can be a meal by itself, is much simpler, but still captures the essence of the original. Cha ca is traditionally cooked at the table.* **Serves 4**

**1** Mix together the *nuoc mam*, salt, and pepper. Add the fish and leave to marinate in the refrigerator for 1 hour.

**2** Pour a generous coating of oil into a frying pan. When hot, add the turmeric and ginger. Mix well, then stir in the pieces of marinated fish. Cook over medium heat for a few minutes. Just before the fish is cooked, add the dill, scallions, and peanuts to the pan and cook for a further 1 minute.

**3** To serve, eat in individual bowls with the vermicelli, herb leaves, and *nuoc cham*.

3 tablespoons *nuoc mam*

1 teaspoon each sea salt and freshly ground black pepper

1 pound river pike or other firm white fish fillets *cut into bite-sized pieces*

vegetable oil for cooking

1 tablespoon ground turmeric

2-inch piece fresh ginger *thinly sliced*

⅓ cup roughly chopped fresh dill

2 tablespoons scallions chopped into 1-inch pieces

2 tablespoons crushed roasted peanuts

8 ounces rice vermicelli *cooked*

leaves of fresh herbs such as mint, cilantro, basil, and Thai basil

*nuoc cham* dipping sauce (see page 22)

# Grilled Prawns

Tom Cang Nuong

*Wonderfully simple, the magic of this dish is in the dip. This is how award-winning Ho Chi Minh City chef, Quach Thien Tuong, serves prawns. Be sure to use the freshest prawns. If you find the dip too tart, add a spoonful of water.* **Serves 4**

**1** Mix the onion and garlic with vegetable oil. Add the prawns and toss to coat. Leave to marinate for at least 3 hours in a cool place, covered.

**2** Grill the prawns over a medium charcoal fire, or cook under a preheated broiler, for about 5 minutes, turning once.

**3** Mix together the sea salt, black pepper, and lime juice in a small dish, and use as a dip for the prawns.

**1 small onion** *minced*

**1 garlic clove** *minced*

**1 teaspoon vegetable oil**

**1 pound raw tiger or king prawns or jumbo shrimp** *peeled and deveined*

For the dip:

**1 teaspoon each sea salt and freshly ground black pepper**

**juice of 1 lime**

# Crab Noodle Soup

Bun Rieu

*For this specialty from the center of Vietnam, the locals traditionally use tiny freshwater crabs, and pound the meat almost to a powder. Some cooks form the crab meat into little patties, but this recipe allows the crab meat to float freely.* **Serves 4 as a complete meal**

**8 shallots** *thinly sliced*

**vegetable oil for frying**

**12 ounces (about 3 cups) crab meat** *flaked*

**6 tomatoes** *roughly chopped*

**2 tablespoons nuoc mam**

**1 teaspoon each sugar and sea salt**

**1 pound fine rice vermicelli** *cooked*

**½ head lettuce** *shredded*

**1 cup beansprouts**

**1 lime** *cut in quarters*

**1** Sauté the shallots in a little hot oil until soft. Add the crab meat, tomatoes, *nuoc mam*, sugar, and salt. Pour in 5 cups water. Bring to a boil, then simmer over low heat for about 30 minutes.

**2** To serve, divide the vermicelli among 4 large individual bowls. Ladle the crab soup over the noodles. Top each serving with a handful each of shredded lettuce and beansprouts and add a squeeze of lime juice.

# Fish Congee

Chao Ca

*The head contains the sweetest meat of a fish, thus making wonderful fish stock for this congee, or rice porridge. If fish head is unavailable, or you have an aversion to looking at fish eyes, you can substitute a second fish fillet.* **Serves 4**

**1** Simmer the fish fillet and fish head in the chicken stock for about 30 minutes. Remove the fillet and head, reserving the stock. Flake the fish fillet into small pieces; discard the fish head.

**2** Place the rice in a hot, dry wok and cook, stirring, for about 5 minutes, or until the rice is beginning to turn yellow.

**3** Add the rice to the stock and season with the *nuoc mam* and ½ teaspoon each salt and pepper. Cook, with minimum stirring, for about 20 minutes, or until the rice is soft but not dry.

**4** Stir in the flaked fish and dill. Serve immediately, sprinkled with freshly ground black pepper.

**6 ounces garoupa (grouper) or other firm white fish fillet**

**1 fish head**

**1 quart chicken stock**

**⅔ cups long-grain white rice**

**1 teaspoon *nuoc mam***

**sea salt and freshly ground black pepper**

**2 tablespoons chopped fresh dill**

# Stuffed Squid

Muc Nhoi Thit

*Stuffing small squid is tricky, but worth the effort. If the squid you buy still have tentacles attached, mince these and add to the filling. This is a recipe recommended by gourmet Aline Ho. It is quite a dry dish so is best served with other, sauced dishes.* **Serves 4–6**

**1 pound young squid** *cleaned and patted dry*

**vegetable oil for frying**

For the filling:

**3 dried Chinese mushrooms** *soaked in warm water for 30 minutes, then minced*

**1 ounce cellophane noodles** *broken into pieces and soaked in warm water for 30 minutes*

**¾ cup ground pork**

**2 shallots** *minced*

**1 garlic clove** *minced*

**2 teaspoons *nuoc mam***

**pinch each of sugar, sea salt, and freshly ground black pepper**

**1** Combine the filling ingredients, mixing well.

**2** Stuff each squid with the filling, packing it in firmly. Secure the opening with a wooden toothpick or sew up with a trussing needle and fine string.

**3** Fry in a little hot oil over medium heat for about 15 minutes or until nicely browned on all sides. After the first few minutes of cooking, pierce the squid with a sharp pointed knife to release any water.

**4** Leave the stuffed squid to cool for a few minutes, then cut them across into ½-inch slices and serve.

# Fish in Claypot
Ca Kho To

*A very traditional dish, this is rich, pungent, and slightly spicy. It should be served with plain steamed rice and, perhaps, as the Vietnamese do, with Hot and Sour Fish Soup (page 18). Use fillets of a firm white fish such as garoupa (grouper), catfish, pike, or halibut. Caramelize the sauce way ahead of time as it needs to cool—and as you may need to wash your hair afterwards, unless your kitchen has very good ventilation.* **Serves 4**

**4 shallots** *thinly sliced*

**2 fresh hot red chilies** *minced*

**freshly ground black pepper**

**1 pound firm, thick white fish fillets**

For the caramel:

**3 tablespoons sugar**

**4 tablespoons** *nuoc mam*

**1** Heat the sugar in a small, heavy-based pan over low heat, stirring constantly, until it has melted and turned to a light golden caramel. Remove from the heat and carefully stir in the *nuoc mam*. Return to the heat and stir for a couple of minutes until the caramel dissolves.

**2** Remove the caramel from the heat again and stir in the shallots and chilies with some freshly ground black pepper. Leave to cool.

**3** Lay the fish fillets in a claypot or in a heavy-bottomed Dutch oven. Pour the sauce over the fish. Cover and cook over low heat for 20–30 minutes, or until the fish flakes easily.

# Grilled Beef with Lemon Grass

Bo Nuong Sa Ot

*The Vietnamese tend to use bamboo skewers for grilling, but metal ones can be utilized instead. The beef tastes delicious dipped in the* nuoc cham, *and can be teamed with a mixed lettuce and herb platter.* **Serves 4**

**1** Combine the marinade ingredients and mix with the beef. Cover and leave in a cool place for at least 2 hours.

**2** Thread the cubes of beef onto skewers, tightly pressed together. Grill over a hot charcoal fire, or cook under a preheated broiler, for about 5 minutes. The edges should be crisp and brown while the inside is just cooked.

**3** Remove the beef from the skewers and serve with *nuoc cham*.

**1 pound filet mignon** *cut into small cubes*

For the marinade:

**4 stalks fresh lemon grass** *minced*

**6 shallots** *minced*

**2 fresh hot red chilies** *minced*

**2 garlic cloves** *minced*

**2 teaspoons vegetable oil**

**1 teaspoon each sea salt and freshly ground black pepper**

To serve:

**nuoc cham dipping sauce (see page 22)**

# Beef Noodle Soup

Pho Bo

*This is one of the best noodle dishes in Southeast Asia, and there are as many versions as there are pho shops in Vietnam. The recipe here is based on one from Chef Dieu Ho in Ho Chi Minh City. Eat with chopsticks and a spoon.* **Serves 4**

**1** To make the broth, bring the stock to boiling point. Add the ginger, cinnamon sticks, coriander seeds, and star anise. Simmer for about 15 minutes. Add the sugar, salt, pepper, and *nuoc mam*. Strain the broth and return to the pan. Keep hot over low heat.

**2** Bring a pan of water to a boil, and warm through fresh noodles or cook rice sticks until *al dente*. Drain and divide among individual bowls. Add a handful of blanched beansprouts and some shallots and cilantro to each bowl, and top with the beef. Ladle the hot broth over (the beef will cook a little in the heat of the broth).

**3** At the table, each diner can add hoisin and chili sauces, lime juice, fresh chili, *ngo gai*, and basil leaves to taste.

**1 pound fresh flat rice noodles or rice sticks**

**8 ounces (2 cups) beansprouts** *blanched briefly to soften slightly*

**8 shallots** *thinly sliced*

**¼ cup minced cilantro**

**8 ounces filet mignon** *thinly sliced*

For the broth:

**7½ cups beef stock or canned beef consommé**

**4-ounce piece fresh ginger** *peeled and smashed*

**2 sticks cinnamon bark**

**½ teaspoon coriander seeds**

**3 pieces star anise**

**1 teaspoon each sugar, sea salt, and freshly ground black pepper**

**4 teaspoons *nuoc mam***

To serve:

**hoisin sauce and chili sauce**

**2 limes** *cut in half*

**2 fresh hot red chilies** *thinly sliced*

**bunch of fresh *ngo gai* (if available)** *torn into pieces*

**bunch of fresh Thai basil**

# Beef in Vinegar Sauce
Bo Nhung Dam

*One of the most famous beef dishes in southern Vietnam, this is one course of seven in the popular* bo bay mon *feast, literally "beef done in seven ways." The sauce should be balanced, with one part vinegar to one part fresh coconut juice (not coconut milk), so measure the coconut juice first. The beef is traditionally dipped into a strong fish paste before eating; use* nuoc mam *as a substitute or simply eat plain.* **Serves 4**

8 ounces filet mignon *thinly sliced*

1 onion *thinly sliced*

For the sauce:

vegetable oil for frying

1 garlic clove *minced*

about 1¼ cups white rice vinegar

2 teaspoons sugar

pinch of sea salt

half the juice from a young coconut

**1** Arrange the beef slices on a plate and pile the onion rings in the center. Place on the table.

**2** Heat a little oil in a small saucepan and lightly brown the garlic. Add the vinegar, sugar, and salt and stir until the mixture comes to a boil. Add the coconut juice and bring back to a boil. Transfer to a fondue pot or similar vessel set over a source of heat to keep the sauce boiling, and bring to the table.

**3** Throw the onion into the boiling sauce, then, using chopsticks, dip the beef into the sauce and cook for about 30 seconds, or according to taste.

# Beef Curry

Bo Xao Lan

*Vietnamese curries are made with freshly ground spice mixtures from the market rather than a paste. The blend of spices for beef curry is similar to Chinese five-spice, though the inclusion of hot mau, from the tiny red-colored nut of an indigenous tree, adds a rich red color (a little tomato paste is an acceptable substitute). Slightly richer than other Vietnamese curries, this dish should be served with rice rather than vermicelli.* **Serves 4**

**1** Combine the five-spice, garlic, chilies, lemon grass, and ½ teaspoon each salt and pepper. Add the beef pieces and mix well. Cover and leave for 1 hour in a cool place to allow the flavors to blend.

**2** Sauté the beef and spices in a little hot oil until browned all over. Add the potatoes and carrots and cook for 2 minutes, stirring. Pour in the coconut milk and beef stock. Bring to a boil, then simmer uncovered over low heat for about 30 minutes, or until the vegetables are softened.

**1 tablespoon five-spice powder**

**1 garlic clove** *minced*

**2 fresh hot red chilies** *minced*

**2 stalks fresh lemon grass** *minced*

**sea salt and freshly ground black pepper**

**8 ounces boneless beef** *diced (about 2 cups)*

**vegetable oil for frying**

**2 medium-sized potatoes** *diced*

**2 carrots** *diced*

**2½ cups coconut milk**

**1¼ cups beef stock**

# Hanoi Charcoal Pork

Bun Cha

*Everyone smells this dish, a specialty of Hanoi, long before they see the store selling it: the pork is grilled outside over hot charcoal, creating a marvelous aroma.* **Serves 4–6**

1 pound boneless pork loin

For the marinade:

1 garlic clove *minced*

2 tablespoons each minced shallots and scallions

2 teaspoons each sugar, *nuoc mam*, and sea salt

2 teaspoons caramel, made from sugar and *nuoc mam* (see Pork in Claypot, page 65)

For the dipping sauce:

2 tablespoons *nuoc mam*

¼ cup lime juice

1 garlic clove *minced*

1 fresh hot red chili *minced*

½ teaspoon sugar

½ carrot *thinly sliced*

½ English cucumber *seeded and thinly sliced*

2 ounces green papaya (if available) *thinly sliced*

To serve:

8 ounces thin rice noodles *cooked*

mustard greens and/or lettuce

beansprouts

sprigs of fresh herbs such as basil, cilantro, and mint

**1** Cut half of the pork loin into pieces about 1-inch square; grind the remaining pork. Mix together the ingredients for the marinade. Divide in half; combine one half with the pork pieces and the other half with the ground pork. Leave in a cool place for at least 1 hour.

**2** Form the ground pork mixture into balls about 1 inch in diameter, and flatten them into patties. Arrange inside a hinged wire grill or on a fine-mesh grill rack together with the pork pieces. Grill over a charcoal fire, or cook under a preheated broiler, until the meat is well browned, turning to cook evenly.

**3** Mix together all the ingredients for the dipping sauce and stir in ½ cup of water.

**4** To serve, place heaps of noodles in individual rice bowls, top with the pork (both patties and pieces), and add torn mustard greens or lettuce leaves, beansprouts, and herbs. Generously spoon the dipping sauce on top to create quite a sloppy dish.

# Fried Pork with Vermicelli

Bun Xao Thit

*Mylinh Lee remembers eating this dish as a child—her mother, To Ha Lee, says it was a quick and easy dish she would rustle up for the children for lunch, using up leftovers. Indeed, the flavors are very simple, but they are appealing to all ages, particularly the blend of hot coconut milk with fresh mint leaves. This is a very light dish.* **Serves 4**

**8 ounces rice vermicelli** *cooked*

**¼ cup roughly chopped fresh mint**

**½ English cucumber** *peeled, seeded, and thinly sliced*

**8 shallots** *thinly sliced*

**2 garlic cloves** *minced*

**vegetable oil for frying**

**8 ounces boneless pork** *chopped into bite-sized pieces (about 2 cups)*

**½ teaspoon each sea salt and freshly ground black pepper**

**1 teaspoon** *nuoc mam*

**1¼ cups coconut milk**

To serve:

**¼ cup crushed roasted peanuts**

*nuoc cham* **dipping sauce (see page 22)**

**1** Divide the vermicelli among 4 bowls and top with the chopped mint and slices of cucumber.

**2** Sauté the shallots and garlic in a little hot oil until soft. Add the pork and season with salt, pepper, and *nuoc mam*. Cook over medium heat, stirring, until the pork is nicely browned.

**3** In a small saucepan, bring the coconut milk to a boil.

**4** Divide the pork mixture and coconut milk among the bowls. Top each serving with crushed peanuts and about 1 tablespoon of *nuoc cham*. Eat immediately, mixing well with chopsticks as you go.

# Grilled Pork with Vermicelli

Banh Hoi Thit Nuong

*This is one of the most common dishes in street-side cafés, though there are no restaurants dedicated entirely to it. The Vietnamese use sheets of fresh vermicelli, but dried vermicelli can be substituted.* **Serves 4**

**1** Combine the marinade ingredients. Add the pork and mix thoroughly. Cover and leave in a cool place for 30 minutes.

**2** Thread the marinated pork slices onto skewers. Grill over a medium charcoal fire, or cook under a preheated broiler, until browned at the edges but still juicy in the center.

**3** To serve, place a handful of lettuce and herbs at the bottom of each of 4 serving bowls and add a pile of vermicelli and a layer of pork slices. Top with a sprinkling of shallots, peanuts, and scallion. Pour *nuoc cham* into the bowls, or use as a dip.

**10 ounces boneless pork** *thinly sliced into medium-sized pieces*

**8 ounces rice vermicelli** *cooked*

For the marinade:

**1 tablespoon minced shallot**

**1 garlic clove** *minced*

**1 teaspoon each** *nuoc mam*, **sugar, and sea salt**

To serve:

**1 head lettuce** *shredded*

**mixed fresh herbs such as mint, cilantro, and basil** *roughly chopped*

**1 tablespoon deep-fried thinly sliced shallots**

**1 tablespoon crushed and roasted peanuts**

**1 tablespoon minced scallion, green part only**

*nuoc cham* **dipping sauce (see page 22)**

# Pork and Shrimp Stew with Pineapple

Tom Thit Xao Dua

*The method of cooking makes the pineapple taste more like a vegetable than a fruit, with all the flavors intermingling for a rich and pungent dish. This recipe comes from Vietnamese food expert Aline Ho. Serve with white rice.* **Serves 2–4**

**1 garlic clove** *minced*

**vegetable oil for frying**

**8 ounces peeled raw medium shrimp**

**5 shallots** *minced*

**8 ounces boneless pork loin** *roughly chopped (about 2 cups)*

**1½ cups peeled fresh pineapple cut into bite-sized pieces**

**4 teaspoons *nuoc mam***

**4 scallions** *minced*

**1 tablespoon minced cilantro**

**1** Toss the garlic into a very hot oiled wok or pan, then add the shrimp. Cook, stirring, for a few minutes or until the shrimp are firm and opaque and the garlic is aromatic. Remove the shrimp from the wok and set aside.

**2** Add the shallots to the hot wok or pan and fry for a couple of minutes to soften, then add the pork pieces. Cook for about 2 minutes, or until browned all over. Drain off any excess liquid. Add the pineapple and *nuoc mam*. Cover and simmer over low heat for about 30 minutes, or until the pineapple is very soft.

**3** Return the garlicky shrimp to the wok along with the scallions and toss until the mixture is warmed through. Serve hot, sprinkled with the chopped cilantro.

# Pork in Claypot
Thit Kho To

*It is hard to believe that this delicious dish was once a staple for peasant paddy-field workers. A heavy-based pan works as well as a traditional claypot.* **Serves 2**

**1** First make the caramel. Heat the sugar in a small, heavy-based pan over low heat, stirring constantly until it is moist and thick. Remove from the heat and carefully add the *nuoc mam*. Return to low heat and stir until the sugar dissolves.

**2** Add the shallots and pepper to the caramel. Leave the sauce to cool.

**3** Pour the sauce into a claypot or heavy-bottomed Dutch oven. Add the pork to the sauce, cover, and simmer for about 30 minutes over low heat, stirring occasionally. At the end of cooking, the pork should be in a little rich gravy. Serve with the hard-boiled egg halves (if using), spooning the gravy over them.

**2 tablespoons chopped shallots**

**½ teaspoon freshly ground black pepper**

**8 ounces boneless pork loin**
*thinly sliced*

**2 eggs** *hard-boiled and halved* **(optional)**

For the caramel:

**3 tablespoons dark brown sugar**

**¼ cup *nuoc mam***

# Stuffed Baguette

Banh Mi Thit

*In Vietnam, the baguette, though thicker and shorter than the best French baguettes, and made without salt, is one of the most endearing and enduring legacies of the French colonial period. Bread is often eaten as an accompaniment to other dishes, but— particularly at breakfast—the Vietnamese like to eat the baguette stuffed with all manner of meats and preserves. Ngu Lan in Ho Chi Minh City is the most famous store for this popular take-out snack. Vietnamese prepared meats, though generally steamed in banana leaf, are very similar to French pâtés and terrines, so the French (or French-style) versions can easily be substituted.* **Serves 3–4**

**1** Open the split baguettes like a book and spread both cut surfaces with butter. Spread one side of each baguette with the liver pâté.

**2** Arrange the sliced pork terrine, shredded chicken, cucumber, chili, pickled carrot and white radish, and the scallion on the other side of each baguette. Squash the baguettes back together, then cut them across into sections and serve immediately.

**2 baguettes** *split down the middle*

**unsalted butter**

**4 ounces soft pork liver pâté**

**4 ounces pork terrine (*cha lua*)** *sliced*

**½–1 cup shredded cooked chicken meat**

**3-inch piece English cucumber** *thinly sliced*

**1 fresh hot red chili** *thinly sliced*

**pickled carrot and white radish (daikon)** *sliced*

**1 scallion** *finely shredded*

# Chicken Noodle Soup
Pho Ga

Pho ga *is not as legendary nor as traditional as* Pho bo *(see page 55), but is today almost as popular. Though not included in this recipe, Vietnamese cooks often add a chicken bouillon cube to the broth for extra flavor.* **Serves 4**

**7½ cups chicken stock**

**4-ounce piece fresh ginger**
*peeled and smashed*

**2 sticks cinnamon bark**

**½ teaspoon coriander seeds**

**3 pieces star anise**

**4 teaspoons *nuoc mam***

**1 teaspoon each sugar, sea salt, and freshly ground black pepper**

**8 shallots** *thinly sliced*

**vegetable oil for frying**

**1 pound fresh flat rice noodles or rice sticks**

**4 scallions, white part only**
*thinly sliced*

**½ onion** *thinly sliced*

**4 ounces cooked chicken meat**

To serve:

**8 ounces (2 cups) beansprouts**
*blanched briefly to soften slightly*

**4 teaspoons each hoisin sauce and chili sauce**

**¼ cup minced cilantro**

**2 fresh hot red chilies** *thinly sliced*

**2 limes** *cut in quarters*

**1** Bring the stock to boiling point. Add the ginger, cinnamon sticks, coriander seeds, and star anise. Simmer for about 15 minutes. Add the *nuoc mam*, sugar, salt, and pepper. Strain the broth and return to the pan. Keep hot over low heat.

**2** Shallow-fry the shallots until soft and beginning to brown. Drain on paper towels and set aside.

**3** Bring a pan of water to a boil, and warm through fresh noodles or cook rice sticks until *al dente*. Drain and divide among individual bowls. Top with fried shallots, scallions, and onion rings, and then chicken, thinly sliced or torn into pieces. Ladle the hot broth into the bowls.

**4** At the table, each diner can add a handful of beansprouts, and hoisin and chili sauces, cilantro, fresh chili, and lime juice to taste.

# Broiled Chicken with Lime Leaf

Ga Nuong La Chanh

*The secret to this recipe, from Hue chef Nuoc Tinh, is to retain moisture in the chicken while it is being broiled. The dish is pungent in both flavor and aroma.* **Serves 4**

**1** Put half of the lime leaves, the scallions, garlic, and 3 tablespoons water in a blender or food processor and whiz until quite smooth. Strain.

**2** Mix the chicken with the honey, *nuoc mam*, a pinch of salt, and ½ teaspoon pepper. Leave to rest for 5 minutes so the flavors can blend.

**3** Combine the chicken mixture with the lime-leaf sauce and leave to marinate for 5 minutes.

**4** Deep-fry the remaining lime-leaf shreds until they turn brown. Remove from the oil and drain on paper towels. Reserve the oil.

**5** Arrange the pieces of chicken close together in a baking pan. Brush with the oil used for frying the lime-leaf shreds. Broil for about 25 minutes, turning the chicken regularly and brushing with any remaining marinade plus lime-leaf oil, until browned on the edges.

**6** Arrange the chicken on a dish and scatter the deep-fried lime-leaf shreds on the top. Eat dipped into *nuoc cham*.

**1 ounce (about 20) makrut lime leaves** *finely shredded*

**2 scallions** *chopped*

**1 garlic clove** *chopped*

**12 ounces skinless boneless chicken** *cut into cubes*

**1 teaspoon honey**

**½ teaspoon *nuoc mam***

**sea salt and freshly ground black pepper**

**vegetable oil for deep-frying**

To serve:

***nuoc cham* dipping sauce (see page 22)**

# Chicken with Lemon Grass

Ga Nuong Xa Ot

*At the end of cooking, most Vietnamese meat dishes have only a little gravy at the bottom.*
**Serves 4**

**2 garlic cloves** *minced*

**2 stalks fresh lemon grass** *minced*

**vegetable oil for frying**

**1 pound skinless boneless chicken breast** *cut into medium-sized pieces*

**½ cup juice from a young coconut**

**2 teaspoons *nuoc mam***

**2 teaspoons ground turmeric**

**1 onion** *roughly chopped*

**2 fresh hot red chilies** *minced*

**pinch of sugar**

**sea salt and freshly ground black pepper**

**1** Gently fry the garlic and half the lemon grass in a little oil, taking care not to let them brown. Add the chicken and stir for a couple of minutes until the pieces are opaque and white on all sides.

**2** Add a little of the coconut juice and stir, then add the *nuoc mam* and turmeric. Stirring all the time, gradually add the remaining coconut juice. Add the onion and cook for about 3 minutes, or until the onion just begins to soften.

**3** Add the remaining lemon grass, the chilies, sugar, ½ teaspoon salt, and a pinch of pepper. Cook for about 2 more minutes, then serve.

# Chicken Congee

Chao Ga

*Vietnamese congee (rice porridge) usually consists of whole grains rather than broken rice grains, hence the initial cooking in a wok.* **Serves 4**

1 whole chicken leg

vegetable oil for frying

1 garlic clove *minced*

⅔ cup long-grain white rice

sea salt and freshly ground black pepper

1 tablespoon minced cilantro

**1** Put the chicken in a saucepan and cover with 1 quart hot water. Bring to a boil, then simmer for about 20 minutes, or until you can penetrate the skin with chopsticks. Remove the chicken and set aside; reserve the chicken stock in the pan. When the chicken is cool, tear the meat into small pieces, discarding skin and bones.

**2** Lightly oil a wok and heat it, then stir in the garlic. After a couple of minutes, add the rice. Cook, stirring, over low heat for about 15 minutes, or until the rice is beginning to turn yellow.

**3** Add the rice to the chicken stock and season with ½ teaspoon each salt and pepper. Cover the pan and cook gently, with minimum stirring, for about 20 minutes, or until the rice is soft but not dry.

**4** Stir in the chicken and serve immediately, sprinkled with freshly ground black pepper and minced cilantro.

# Chicken Rice in Claypot

Com Ga Hanoi

*To make this dish successfully, there must be no excess liquid in the rice and chicken (the steaming ensures that the dish is not dry), and the cooking of the two components should be timed so they are ready at the same time. Any burnt rice left on the bottom of the pan is considered a delicacy in Vietnam.* **Serves 2 as a complete meal**

**1** Heat a little oil in a claypot, or in a heavy-bottomed Dutch oven, and sauté the shallots and half the garlic until soft. Add the rice and cook, stirring, until it is lightly browned.

**2** Add the chicken stock. Bring to a boil, then cover the claypot and cook, without stirring, for 10–12 minutes, or until the rice is tender and all the liquid has been absorbed.

**3** Meanwhile, heat a little oil in a frying pan and sauté the remaining garlic until soft. Add the chicken and stir until white and opaque. Add the remaining ingredients. Cook for 5–10 minutes, or until the chicken is cooked through, stirring occasionally.

**4** Pile the chicken mixture on top of the rice. Cover the claypot and continue cooking for about 2 minutes, then bring to the table and serve.

**vegetable oil for frying**

**2 shallots** *minced*

**2 garlic cloves** *minced*

**⅔ cup long-grain white rice**

**1½ cups chicken stock**

**12 ounces boneless chicken** *diced*

**1 tablespoon chopped scallion**

**2 ounces fresh or canned straw mushrooms**

**4 dried Chinese mushrooms** *soaked in warm water for 30 minutes, then minced*

**1 teaspoon *nuoc mam***

**½ teaspoon each sugar and sea salt**

# Southern Vietnamese Chicken Curry

Ca Ri Ga

*Vietnamese chicken curry is neither Thai, Indian, nor Chinese in style—do not expect heat or intensity, or even subtlety. Instead, you will have a rather heady, aromatic dish. Throw a handful of freshly torn Thai basil on top with some freshly ground black pepper to bring out the fragrance. Serve with rice vermicelli rather than rice for added interest.* **Serves 4**

**1** Shallow-fry the potato pieces in hot oil until lightly browned. Drain on paper towels and set aside.

**2** Heat a little oil in a pan and sauté the shallots with the lemon grass, garlic, and chilies until soft. Add the curry powder and stir for 2 minutes. Add the chicken and cook, stirring, until it is opaque.

**3** Add the potatoes, salt, coconut milk, and chicken stock. Bring to a boil, then cover and simmer gently for about 30 minutes. Garnish with Thai basil leaves, if using.

**2 medium-sized potatoes** *cut into chunks*

**vegetable oil for frying**

**8 shallots** *minced*

**4 stalks fresh lemon grass** *minced*

**2 garlic cloves** *minced*

**2 fresh hot red chilies** *minced*

**2 tablespoons mild Indian curry powder**

**1 pound skinless boneless chicken breast** *chopped into bite-sized pieces*

**1 teaspoon sea salt**

**1¼ cups coconut milk**

**2½ cups chicken stock**

**fresh Thai basil leaves (optional)**

# Vegetable Curry

Ca Ri Chay

*As a main dish, this is deliciously subtle to the point of comfort food. Eat with rice vermicelli or a baguette.* **Serves 2–4**

**vegetable oil for frying**

**1 cup diced taro root**

**1 cup thinly sliced leek**

**2 carrots** *diced*

**2 ounces fresh or canned straw mushrooms**

**1 tablespoon mild Indian curry powder**

**5 stalks fresh lemon grass** *cut into 1-inch lengths and crushed*

**½ teaspoon sugar**

**sea salt and freshly ground black pepper**

**1¼ cups vegetable stock**

**1½ cups coconut milk**

**1 pound firm beancurd (tofu)** *cut into 1-inch cubes*

**1** Heat a little oil in a large saucepan and add the taro, leek, carrots, and mushrooms. Cook, stirring, for 2 minutes. Add the curry powder, lemon grass, sugar, 1 teaspoon salt, and ½ teaspoon pepper and stir well to mix. Pour in the stock and 1 cup of the coconut milk. Bring to a boil, then cover and simmer for about 20 minutes, or until all the vegetables are soft.

**2** Meanwhile, deep-fry the cubes of beancurd until they are golden brown all over. Drain on paper towels.

**3** Add the beancurd to the curry along with the remaining coconut milk. Cover and cook for a further 2 minutes. Serve hot.

# Duck Steamboat

Lau Vit

*At a Ho Chi Minh City restaurant that specializes in duck dishes, this hotpot is the most popular item on the menu. Individual gas burners are placed on the tables, to keep the stock boiling. Goat hotpot, cooked in exactly the same way, is also extremely popular.* **Serves 4–6**

**1** Put the duck in a shallow pan, cover with some of the chicken stock, and simmer with the lid on for about 45 minutes, or until cooked and tender. Drain and cut into thick slices, discarding the skin if preferred.

**2** Cook the chunks of taro in boiling water for about 15 minutes or until they are soft. Drain.

**3** Pile the dried noodles and vegetables on a plate and bring to the table. Bring the remaining stock to a boil, then pour 1 quart into a steamboat, meat fondue pot, or other large, heavy-based pan that can be set over a source of heat on the table. Add the sliced duck, cooked taro, and scallions.

**4** To eat, cook the vegetables and noodles in the stock, and eat everything together. Add more stock as necessary.

**2 boneless duck breasts**

**about 7½ cups chicken stock**

**1 taro root (about 1 pound)**
*chopped into chunks*

**bunch of scallions, white part only**
*cut into 1-inch pieces*

To serve:

**8 ounces dried thin egg noodles**

**1 pound mustard greens**

**1 pound water spinach (or use spinach or chard)**

**Chinese chives, leaves only (if available)**

# Braised Duck Breast with Pineapple

Vit Ham Thom

*This recipe includes a little* nuoc mam, *the most widely used seasoning in Vietnamese cooking, and in combination with the remaining ingredients it makes a dish that is pleasing to all tastes. Serve it with plain rice or a baguette.* **Serves 4–6**

**10 ounces skinless boneless duck breast** *chopped into pieces*

**8 shallots** *minced*

**2 garlic cloves** *minced*

**1 tablespoon *nuoc mam***

**sea salt and freshly ground black pepper**

**vegetable oil for frying**

**2 onions** *roughly chopped*

**8 dried Chinese mushrooms** *soaked in warm water for 30 minutes, then thinly sliced*

**2 fresh hot red chilies** *minced*

**2½ cups chicken stock**

**1½ cups peeled fresh pineapple cut into small chunks**

**1** Mix the duck with the shallots, garlic, *nuoc mam*, and ½ teaspoon each salt and pepper. Cover and leave for 1 hour in a cool place to allow the flavors to blend.

**2** Heat a little oil in a wok or sauté pan and sauté the duck mixture for 2–3 minutes or until the shallots are soft. Add the onions, mushrooms, and chilies and cook, stirring, for another 2 minutes. Add the chicken stock and pineapple and stir. Bring to a boil, then simmer for about 40 minutes, or until both the duck and the pineapple are tender.

# Hue-Style Noodles

Bun Bo Hue

*Unusual in its combination of beef and pork, this is one of the most readily available dishes in Hue, the old Imperial capital of Vietnam. Locals are often seen eating it with a baguette. Less rich agriculturally than either the south or the north, the one thing that grows with abandon in Hue is chilies, and these are added liberally to this dish. The Vietnamese eat the fresh ham hocks, but you can add more boneless pork instead if you prefer, or simply use leftover reheated roast beef and pork. Banana flower adds a crisp texture and slightly starchy flavor.* **Serves 4**

**1 pound fresh ham hocks or pork bones**

**6 stalks fresh lemon grass** *cut into 2-inch pieces and crushed*

**2 tablespoons *nuoc mam***

**1 teaspoon each sugar, sea salt, and freshly ground black pepper**

**4 ounces each boneless beef shank and pork loin**

**1 pound large round rice noodles** *cooked*

**1 cup beansprouts**

To serve:

**sprigs of fresh herbs such as basil, Thai basil, cilantro, and mint**

**2 ounces banana flower (if available)** *thinly sliced*

**4 teaspoons chili paste or chili sauce**

**4 fresh hot red chilies** *thinly sliced diagonally*

**1 lime** *cut into quarters*

**1** Bring 2½ quarts water to a boil. Add the fresh ham hocks or pork bones and lemon grass. Boil for about 10 minutes, skimming constantly, then cover the pan and simmer for 1½ hours.

**2** Strain the broth. Keep the ham hocks to one side if you are eating them. Add the *nuoc mam*, sugar, salt, and pepper to the broth and bring back to a simmer. Cook the beef shank and pork loin in the broth for 10–15 minutes until cooked and tender. Remove the meat. Thinly slice the shank and cut the pork into small pieces.

**3** To serve, place a pile of noodles in each large individual bowl, top with some beansprouts, pork, and beef, and ladle the broth over. Before eating, add a handful of herbs, the banana flower, if using, the chili paste or sauce, chilies, and lime juice to taste.

# Haiphong Noodles

## Mi Xao Haiphong

*This noodle creation is a traditional dish from the port city of Haiphong. The method of preparation, which is rapid stir-frying in a very hot oiled wok, indicates how Chinese cooking methods have influenced Vietnamese cuisine, particularly in the north.* **Serves 2–4**

**1** Heat a wok, add a little oil, and, when very hot, add the garlic and shallots. Stir fry rapidly for about 30 seconds. Add the egg and stir for about 30 more seconds. Add the chicken and pork and stir until seared. Add the shrimp, beansprouts, green bell pepper, chili, and scallions, continuing to stir-fry until the shrimp are just firm. Add the sesame oil and *nuoc mam*.

**2** Moisten the noodles with warm water to prevent them from sticking together, then throw them in batches into the wok with a pinch of salt, stirring and tossing to combine the ingredients thoroughly. When the noodles are hot, serve immediately, with sprigs of fresh cilantro on top.

**vegetable oil for frying**

**1 garlic clove** *minced*

**5 shallots** *thinly sliced*

**1 egg** *beaten*

**2 ounces (about ⅓ cup) each diced boneless chicken and pork**

**2 ounces peeled raw medium shrimp**

**¼ cup beansprouts**

**1 green bell pepper** *thinly sliced*

**1 fresh hot red chili** *thinly sliced diagonally*

**3 scallions** *cut into 1-inch lengths*

**½ teaspoon each Asian sesame oil and** *nuoc mam*

**6 ounces thin round egg noodles** *cooked*

**pinch of sea salt**

**sprigs of cilantro for garnish**

# SIDE
## DISHES

# Grilled Eggplant with Soy Sauce
Ca Nuong

*The Vietnamese often top grilled eggplant with crab meat or ground beef. This is almost a vegetarian version, given a sprinkling of* nuoc mam. **Serves 2–4**

2 **Asian eggplants**

4 **scallions** *minced*

2 **tablespoons vegetable oil**

4 **teaspoons soy sauce**

½ **teaspoon** *nuoc mam*

**1** Prick the eggplants in several places with a fork, then grill over a charcoal fire for about 20 minutes, or until the flesh is soft but before the skin burns. When cool enough to handle, peel the eggplants and cut them in half lengthwise.

**2** Put the scallions into a bowl. Heat the oil in a pan until very hot, then pour it over the scallions. Immediately drain the scallions.

**3** Sprinkle the scallions over the eggplants, then gently pour the soy sauce and *nuoc mam* on top. Serve.

# Braised Straw Mushrooms in Claypot

Nam Rom Kho To

*This dish is simple to make but complex in flavor, and is an excellent example of how the Vietnamese use soy sauce to produce a dish quite different from anything Chinese. Firm, with an almost earthy flavor, fresh straw mushrooms are not always easy to find outside Asia, so use canned if necessary. With their unique cone shape, they are difficult to replace with another variety of mushroom. Matching Asian food with wine is often a problem, but this dish goes well with a big red wine such as a Syrah from the northern Rhone.* **Serves 4**

vegetable oil for cooking

2 garlic cloves *minced*

8 ounces fresh or canned straw mushrooms

¼ cup soy sauce

2 tablespoons sugar

1 teaspoon each sea salt and freshly ground black pepper

**1** Heat a little oil in a claypot or heavy-bottomed pan and soften the garlic. Add the mushrooms and cook, stirring, for 1 minute.

**2** Add the rest of the ingredients. Cover and simmer over low heat for about 10 minutes.

# Stir-Fried Morning Glory

## Rau Muong Xao Toi

*Morning glory (rau muong), similar to Chinese water spinach (ong choi), is the most popular vegetable in Vietnam, and one of the few to be cooked in such a simple manner. Substitute regular spinach if the Asian vegetables are not available, and reduce the amount of garlic if the taste seems too pungent.* **Serves 2–4**

**1** Blanch the morning glory or spinach in a large pan of boiling water for 30 seconds, then drain.

**2** Heat a wok, add a little oil, and then sauté the garlic for about 30 seconds. Add the morning glory and stir-fry for about 30 seconds or until soft. Serve immediately.

**1 pound morning glory (or use spinach leaves)**

**vegetable oil for frying**

**4 garlic cloves** *minced*

# Rice with Omelet

Com Chien Hoang Bao

*The Vietnamese name for this dish translates as "The Emperor's Coat," yellow being the traditional regal color. Typical of dishes from Hue, it contains simple ingredients, but is thought to look very special.* **Serves 2–4**

**1** Stir-fry the onion with the garlic and lemon grass in an oiled wok over high heat. Add the mixed vegetables and the rice and fry, stirring continually with a spatula, until the vegetables are soft. Remove from the heat and keep warm.

**2** Season the eggs with the salt and pepper. Heat a little oil in a 10-inch frying pan, pour in the eggs, and cook until the omelet is nicely browned on the base.

**3** Spoon the rice and vegetables into a mound on a plate. Lay the omelet over the rice mound, browned side up, and top with fresh cilantro. Serve immediately.

**1 onion** *minced*

**1 garlic clove** *minced*

**1 stalk fresh lemon grass** *minced*

**vegetable oil for frying**

**8 ounces (about 2 cups) mixed finely diced carrot, finely diced Asian turnip (or regular turnip), shelled peas, and corn kernels**

**²/₃ cup long-grain white rice** *cooked*

**bunch of cilantro sprigs**

For the omelet:

**2 eggs** *beaten*

**pinch each of sea salt and freshly ground black pepper**

# Fried Rice with Lemon Grass and Shrimp

Com Huong Giang

*With its lemon-grass flavoring, this is obviously not a typical Chinese-style fried rice. However, it is cooked in the same way as it would be in a Cantonese kitchen—in a wok over a fierce heat.* **Serves 2**

**vegetable oil for frying**

**2 stalks fresh lemon grass** *minced*

**4 shallots** *minced*

**1 fresh hot red chili** *minced*

**½ teaspoon sea salt**

**4 ounces peeled raw small shrimp**

**1 cup long-grain white rice** *cooked*

**1** Heat a wok over high heat, then add a little oil and stir-fry the lemon grass, shallots, chili, and salt for 1 minute. Add the shrimp and stir-fry for about 1 minute, or until they are firm.

**2** Add the cooked rice to the wok. Toss everything together until heated through, then serve immediately.

# Vermicelli with Shallots

Banh Hoi

*In Vietnam, a plate of warm vermicelli in the center of the table is as popular as a bowl of rice, even as an accompaniment for dishes with rich sauces like curries. Cold vermicelli can be warmed up easily in a microwave oven.* **Serves 4–6**

**1** Cook the vermicelli in boiling water until *al dente*.

**2** Meanwhile, deep-fry the shallots in hot oil until golden brown. Drain on paper towels.

**3** Drain the vermicelli, scatter the shallots over the top, and garnish with cilantro. Bring to the table immediately.

**8 ounces rice vermicelli**

**8 shallots** *thinly sliced*

**vegetable oil for deep-frying**

**sprigs of cilantro**

# Okra with Shallots

Dau Bap Hap

*This simple vegetable goes well with rich curries and caramelized dishes such as Fish in Claypot (page 52).* **Serves 4–6**

**6 shallots** *thinly sliced*

**vegetable oil for deep-frying**

**8 ounces okra**

**soy sauce to serve**

**1** Deep-fry the thinly sliced shallots in hot oil until golden brown. Drain on paper towels.

**2** Cook the okra whole in a little water in a covered pan for about 5 minutes or until tender. Drain. Top with the deep-fried shallots and serve dipped into soy sauce.

# Stuffed Chinese Bitter Melon

Hu Gua Ham

*The Vietnamese, like the Chinese, are enthusiastic about bitter flavors, which are not as popular in Western cuisines. This dish may not be immediately accessible, therefore, but it is a sophisticated and unusual dish well worth trying.* **Serves 4–6**

**1** Carefully make a slit down the length of each bitter melon, and remove all seeds and pith from the center. Blanch in boiling water for about 2 minutes. Drain and leave to cool slightly.

**2** Combine all the remaining ingredients, except the *nuoc mam*, mixing very thoroughly. Pack this filling tightly into the melons.

**3** Place the stuffed melons in fresh boiling water and simmer for about 30 minutes or until the skin is soft and the filling set. Add the *nuoc mam* to the cooking water and simmer for a further 5 minutes.

**4** Remove from the pan and allow to cool slightly before cutting across into slices about ½ inch wide. Serve warm.

**2 Chinese bitter melons (6 inches long)**

**¾ cup ground pork**

**1 garlic clove** *minced*

**2 shallots** *minced*

**6 dried Chinese mushrooms** *soaked in warm water for 30 minutes, then minced*

**½ ounce cellophane noodles** *finely chopped*

**½ teaspoon each sugar, sea salt, and freshly ground black pepper**

**1 teaspoon** *nuoc mam*

# Deep-Fried Beancurd with Lemon Grass
Dau Phu Chien Xa Ot

*Beancurd is relatively fragile and needs to be treated gently. Drain it carefully and fry just a few pieces at a time, handling with two spatulas. The dish is dry, so serve with other dishes that are moist.* **Serves 2–4**

**1 pound firm beancurd (tofu)**
*cut into 1-inch cubes*

**¼ cup minced fresh lemon grass**

**2 fresh hot red chilies** *minced*

**½ teaspoon sea salt**

**vegetable oil for deep-frying**

**2 garlic cloves** *minced*

**1** Drain the beancurd cubes on paper towels.

**2** Mix together the lemon grass, chilies, and salt. Gently toss with the beancurd, then cover and leave for 30 minutes to blend the flavors.

**3** Deep-fry the beancurd in hot oil for about 10 minutes, or until golden brown all over. Drain on paper towels and keep warm.

**4** Stir the garlic into the remaining lemon-grass mixture. Sauté the mixture in a little hot oil until the lemon grass is golden. Pile on top of the beancurd and serve immediately.

# Stewed Beancurd with Tomato and Eggplant

Dau Phu Rim Ca Chua

*Aline Ho, who demonstrated how to prepare this dish, stresses that it is very subtle, relying on the* nuoc mam *to elevate it to something special (you don't even need to add salt). Use long, thin Asian eggplants that look attractive and require no prior salting.* **Serves 4–6**

**1 pound firm beancurd (tofu)** *cut into 1-inch cubes*

**vegetable oil for deep-frying**

**1 onion** *roughly chopped*

**1 pound tomatoes** *roughly chopped*

**12 ounces Asian eggplants** *cut across into ½ inch slices*

**1 tablespoon *nuoc mam***

**½ teaspoon sugar**

**1** Drain the beancurd on paper towels, then deep-fry until golden brown all over (about 10 minutes). Drain well and set aside.

**2** Sauté the onion in a little hot oil until beginning to soften. Add the tomatoes and cook for about 10 minutes, or until the tomatoes have broken down into a pulp, stirring frequently.

**3** Add the eggplants, *nuoc mam*, and sugar and stir well. Cover the pan and cook until the eggplant slices are soft. Add the beancurd and warm through, then serve.

# Green Mango Salad

Goi Xoai

*A simple but delicious side dish, this is often served with Vietnamese street foods. Modern recipes add ingredients like grilled shrimp, but this is the dish in its basic form.*
**Serves 4–6**

**1** Peel the mangoes, then cut them into long thin shreds. (The Vietnamese have an ingenious little wooden shredder that creates long thin shreds; to achieve the same result you can use a sharp knife—cut into the flesh repeatedly from top to bottom and then thinly shave off the flesh.)

**2** Combine all the ingredients, and serve immediately.

**2 green mangoes**

**1 fresh hot red chili** *thinly sliced*

**1 tablespoon minced fresh Thai basil**

**1 teaspoon** *nuoc mam*

# Green Papaya and Beef Salad

Bo Du Du

*Green papaya has little flavor of its own, but is the perfect backdrop to other ingredients. There are a number of methods for creating the dried beef; this one comes from Hanoi-born chef Nguyen Anh Son.* **Serves 4–6**

**1** Put the steak in a dish. Mix together the other ingredients, pour over the beef, and turn to coat. Leave to marinate in a cool place for 2 hours. Roast in a preheated oven at 210°F for about 1 hour. Cool the steak, then slice it thinly.

**2** Combine the ingredients for the dressing in a mixing bowl.

**3** Add the papaya, carrot, and cilantro to the dressing and toss together by hand. Transfer to a serving dish, leaving behind any excess liquid. Mix in the beef strips.

**4** Top with the crushed roasted peanuts and serve immediately.

**1 green papaya** *peeled and cut into long thin shreds*

**1 carrot** *grated*

**1 tablespoon minced cilantro**

**2 teaspoons crushed roasted peanuts**

For the beef:

**6 ounces boneless sirloin steak**

**1 teaspoon honey**

**pinch each of sea salt and freshly ground black pepper**

**1 garlic clove** *minced*

**1 shallot** *minced*

**1 stalk fresh lemon grass** *minced*

**1 fresh hot red chili** *minced*

**½ teaspoon five-spice powder**

For the dressing:

**1 garlic clove** *minced*

**½ teaspoon sea salt**

**1 teaspoon sugar**

**½ cup white rice vinegar**

**1 fresh hot red chili** *minced*

# Chicken and Lemon Leaf Salad

Ga Xe Phay

*Vietnamese salads must be served extremely fresh or they lose their texture and become soggy. The Vietnamese use* rau ram *in this classic dish; mint is the best alternative. Lemon leaf adds texture as much as flavor, but can be omitted if necessary, as it is not always easy to find.* **Serves 4–6**

**8 ounces boneless chicken** *shredded*

**½ onion** *thinly sliced*

**½ English cucumber** *seeded and thinly sliced*

**1 cup beansprouts**

**6 tablespoons minced fresh mint**

**4 fresh lemon leaves (if available)** *shredded*

For the dressing:

**juice of 3 limes**

**½ teaspoon sea salt**

**1 teaspoon sugar**

**1** Combine the ingredients for the dressing, stirring well, and set aside.

**2** Mix together the chicken, onion, cucumber, beansprouts, fresh mint, and lemon leaves. Toss with the dressing and serve immediately.

# Chicken and Cabbage Salad

Goi Ga Bap Cai

*Bright and lively in flavor, this dish is extremely popular all over the country. The Vietnamese name translates as "torn" chicken: for the best effect, tear the chicken by hand rather than cutting it with a knife. Napa cabbage works better than a crisp, tight white cabbage.* **Serves 4**

**1** Tear the chicken into bite-size pieces and put in a bowl.

**2** Add all the remaining ingredients. Toss together with your hands, then discard any excess liquid. Serve immediately.

**6 ounces boneless chicken** *grilled or poached*

**8 ounces Napa cabbage** *cut across in fine shreds (about 3 cups)*

**1 small onion** *very thinly sliced into rings*

**juice of 2 limes**

**2 tablespoons minced fresh mint**

**1 teaspoon freshly ground black pepper**

**pinch of sea salt**

# Lotus Salad

Goi Ngo Sen

*The stem, or root, of the aquatic lotus plant is deliciously crisp and fresh tasting, and is further enhanced by the addition of lime juice and fresh chili and herbs. Use lotus bulb if stems are unavailable. The Vietnamese use the herb* rau ram, *but Thai basil is a good substitute.* **Serves 2–4**

**8 ounces fresh lotus stem or bulb** *finely sliced*

**3 tablespoons minced fresh Thai basil**

**1 carrot** *cut into very fine sticks*

**4 ounces boneless chicken** *shredded (about 1 cup)*

**1 fresh hot red chili** *thinly sliced*

For the dressing:

**½ teaspoon sugar**

**pinch of sea salt**

**juice of 2 limes**

To serve:

**1 tablespoon chopped roasted peanuts**

**1 tablespoon deep-fried thinly sliced shallots**

**sprigs of cilantro**

**1** Carefully mix together the lotus stem, basil, carrot, chicken, and chili, using chopsticks to prevent the ingredients from breaking up.

**2** Stir the sugar and salt into the lime juice, then pour over the salad and gently mix together.

**3** Sprinkle the peanuts and shallots over the salad, top with torn cilantro leaves, and serve immediately.

# Bamboo Shoot Salad

## Goi Mang

*When in season, fresh bamboo shoots are sometimes used to make this salad. However, as they are difficult to prepare, canned shoots are more commonly used and work very well for this recipe.* **Serves 4–6**

**2 cups canned bamboo shoots cut into very fine sticks**

**6 ounces sirloin steak** *prepared as in Step 1, Green Papaya and Beef Salad (page 101)*

**¼ cup minced fresh Thai basil**

**2 teaspoons each *nuoc mam* and lime juice**

**½ teaspoon sea salt**

**2 tablespoons white sesame seeds**

**1** Heat the bamboo shoots in a little simmering water. Drain, then transfer to a warmed serving dish.

**2** Add the beef, basil, *nuoc mam*, lime juice, and salt and toss well together. Top with the sesame seeds and serve while the bamboo shoots are still warm.

# Grapefruit Salad

Goi Buoi

*The off-sour taste of grapefruit combined with the sweetness of shrimp makes for a light and refreshing salad, which is particularly good in the summer. A more traditional version of the recipe uses dried, flaked squid.* **Serves 4**

**1** Combine the grapefruit, shrimp, cilantro, and *nuoc cham*, mixing gently.

**2** Serve immediately, topped with the peanuts.

2½–3 cups peeled grapefruit broken into bite-sized pieces

4 ounces peeled cooked small shrimp

2 tablespoons roughly chopped cilantro

1 teaspoon *nuoc cham* dipping sauce (see page 22)

1 tablespoon chopped roasted peanuts

# DESSERTS

## AND DRINKS

# Sweet Dumplings in Ginger Syrup

Che Xoi Nuoc

*The secret of success here is to have a pliable dough and to press it as thin as possible without it tearing. The syrup is extremely sweet, but the heat of the ginger and the richness of the coconut milk combine for a delicious experience.* **Makes about 12 dumplings**

For the filling:

**⅔ cup dried yellow beans or ½ cup split peas** *soaked overnight*

**1 tablespoon vegetable oil (ideally oil in which shallots have been deep-fried)**

**1 teaspoon sugar**

For the dough:

**5 cups rice flour**

For the syrup:

**2¾ cups sugar**

**1 tablespoon shredded fresh ginger**

For the coconut sauce:

**1¾ cups coconut milk**

**2 teaspoons sugar**

**pinch of sea salt**

**8 teaspoons cornstarch mixed with 8 teaspoons water**

For the topping:

**3 tablespoons white sesame seeds**

**1** To make the filling, cook the yellow beans or split peas in boiling water for about 45–60 minutes or until very soft. Drain and mash. Add the oil and sugar, to create a thick paste. Set aside.

**2** Put the rice flour in a bowl and make a well in the center. Gradually add enough warm water to make a smooth, pliable dough (about 2 cups). Take small chunks of dough and flatten each into a palm-sized circle. Place a teaspoon of filling in the center of each circle and squeeze together the edges at the top to make a ball. Discard excess dough to avoid thick overlaps (use these pieces to make small balls with no stuffing).

**3** Add the dumplings to a pan of boiling water. They will rise to the surface when they are cooked, about 15–20 minutes. Drain and plunge immediately into cold water. Drain again.

**4** For the syrup, combine the sugar, ginger, and 1 quart water in a saucepan and bring to a boil.

**5** In another pan, bring the coconut milk to a boil. Add the sugar and salt, then slowly add the cornstarch mixture, stirring until just thickened. The sauce should be quite runny. To serve, place one or two large dumplings and a few small ones in each bowl. Pour hot ginger syrup over the top, add 1–2 tablespoons of hot coconut sauce, and sprinkle with sesame seeds.

# Banana Fritters

## Chuoi Chien

*This delicious little snack is frequently prepared along village streets, where women set up stalls in front of their houses. In Vietnam, cooks would use the small, broad Thai cooking bananas.* **Serves 4–6**

**6 tablespoons all-purpose flour**

**2 tablespoons sugar**

**1 egg** *beaten*

**¼ cup milk**

**1½ pounds (4–5 medium) bananas**

**vegetable oil for frying**

**1** Mix together the flour, sugar, egg, and milk to make a smooth paste-like batter. Leave to rest for 1 hour.

**2** Slice each banana in half lengthwise, then across into chunks about 3 inches long.

**3** Dip the banana pieces into the batter and shallow-fry in hot oil for a few minutes or until golden brown all over. Drain quickly on a wire rack and serve warm.

# Banana in Coconut Milk with Sago

Che Chuoi

*Huge pots of this pudding can be spotted in the markets, alongside tiny little crème caramels and brightly colored coconut-milk drinks layered with fruit gelatin, beans, and ice—all are particularly popular with young Vietnamese women. The banana pudding is eaten most often mid-morning or mid-afternoon, rather than after a meal.* **Serves 4**

**1** Soak the sago in cool water for about 10 minutes. Drain.

**2** Combine the coconut milk, sugar, and 1¼ cups water in a pan and bring to a boil.

**3** Cut each banana in half lengthwise, then across into pieces about 2 inches long. Add the bananas and sago to the coconut mixture and cook, stirring occasionally, for about 10 minutes, or until the sago is translucent and the bananas soft. Serve warm.

⅓ cup pearl sago (or use tapioca)

1¾ cups coconut milk

¼ cup sugar

1 pound (about 3 medium) bananas

# Coconut Crème Caramel

Banh Flan

*Crème caramel, often with a coconut flavor as in this recipe, is so popular in Vietnam that it is considered to be a Vietnamese recipe rather than French—it is available everywhere, from market stalls to upmarket restaurants. This recipe comes from a chef at the Omni Saigon hotel.* **Serves 4**

**1** Put ⅔ cup of the sugar in a heavy-based saucepan and add ½ cup water. Bring to a boil, stirring to dissolve the sugar. Boil until the mixture caramelizes to a golden brown. Remove from the heat and add another 2 tablespoons water, stirring until all the caramel has dissolved. Divide the caramel among 4 ramekins, each about 3½ inches in diameter.

**2** Combine the milk and coconut milk in a saucepan and heat until bubbles appear around the edge. Remove from the heat and whisk in the eggs, remaining sugar, and vanilla extract. Add the coconut. Divide among the ramekins.

**3** Half-fill a roasting pan with water, place a rack on top, and set the ramekins on the rack. Bake in a preheated oven at 325°F for about 40 minutes. Leave to cool. Loosen the edges, then turn out of the ramekins for serving.

**1 cup sugar**

**1 cup milk**

**1 cup coconut milk**

**4 eggs** *beaten*

**a few drops of pure vanilla extract**

**⅓ cup freshly grated coconut or dried shredded coconut**

# Beancurd in Ginger Sauce

Che Dau Hu

*Traditionally, the beancurd for this dish would have been made at home using soybeans, flour, and gypsum powder. Today almost no one has the time to do that, and a ready-prepared beancurd is used.* **Serves 4**

**1 pound beancurd (tofu)**

**¼ cup packed brown sugar**

**1-inch piece fresh ginger**
*finely grated*

**½ lime**

**1** Slice the beancurd and divide among four bowls.

**2** Combine the sugar and 1 cup water in a pan and bring to a boil. Add the ginger and stir for about 1 minute, then pour the ginger syrup over the beancurd. Top with a squeeze of lime juice and eat.

# Black Sticky Rice

Xoi Nep Than

*When cooked, black glutinous rice retains more texture than white glutinous rice, which means this dessert never turns into a mush.* **Serves 4**

**1** Rinse and drain the rice, then mix with the beans. Steam for about 1 hour or until everything is soft.

**2** Transfer to a dish. Add the sugar and mix thoroughly, then stir in the coconut milk. Serve warm.

**1 pound (about 2¼ cups) black glutinous rice** *soaked overnight*

**4 ounces (about ½ cup) dried Chinese red beans** *soaked overnight*

**2 tablespoons sugar**

**3 tablespoons coconut milk**

# Fruit with Cinnamon and Lime Dressing
Trai Cay

*The Vietnamese tend to eat only one fruit at a time—the one at the height of its season. Fruits such as strawberries and cherries grow in the cooler climate of Dalat, toward the center of Vietnam, but tropical fruits are more widely available. Dragon fruit comes from the coastal city of Nha Trang. For a simpler presentation, omit the dressing and just serve with lime wedges, to be squeezed over the fruit at the table.* **Serves 6**

**a selection of fruit such as mango, papaya, banana, dragon fruit, pineapple, star fruit, watermelon, and honeydew melon**

For the dressing:

**grated zest and juice of 6 limes**

**3 tablespoons honey**

**½ teaspoon Asian sesame oil**

**1 teaspoon ground cinnamon**

**pinch of sea salt**

**1** Cut the fruit into chunky slices, peeling it if necessary, and arrange on a plate or in a bowl.

**2** Combine the lime zest and juice in a bowl (you need about ⅔ cup juice). Gradually add the honey, stirring, to make a creamy mixture. Taste and add a little more honey if the dressing is too sharp. Stir in the sesame oil, cinnamon, and salt.

**3** Pour the dressing over the fruit and stir gently to combine. Leave in a cool place for about 15 minutes, to allow the flavors to develop, then serve.

# Banana Bread Pudding

Banh Chuoi Nuong

*There are various versions of this popular pudding, including one that uses condensed milk in combination with coconut milk. Some puddings end up quite dry; this one is deliciously soft and moist.* **Serves 4–6**

¾ **cup coconut milk**

½ **teaspoon pure vanilla extract**

**8 slices white bread** *crusts removed*

**butter for greasing**

**1½ pounds (4–5 medium) ripe bananas** *sliced diagonally*

½ **cup packed brown sugar**

**1** Combine the coconut milk and vanilla extract in a shallow bowl. Add the bread and leave to soak for 10 minutes.

**2** Grease an 8-inch nonstick baking pan with a little butter. Layer the moistened slices of bread, the bananas, and sugar in the pan, starting with bread and finishing with bananas sprinkled with sugar.

**3** Bake in a preheated oven at 350°F for about 30 minutes. Leave to cool for at least 3 hours before unmolding.

# Yogurt

Yaourt

*Signs all over Vietnamese towns advertising "yaourt" testify to the popularity of French yogurt. The yogurt made in Vietnam is thick, rich, and creamy, closer to the Greek style.*

**Serves 4**

**1** Mix together the topping ingredients.

**2** Divide the yogurt among 4 bowls and sprinkle over the topping.

**4 cups strained plain yogurt**

For the topping:

**handful of golden raisins**

**handful of roasted unsalted peanuts** *crushed*

**handful of roasted unsalted cashew nuts** *crushed*

**handful of chopped candied peel**

**4 candied cherries** *minced*

# Kir

Kir

*A classic French drink is given a lively Vietnamese twist. Inexpensive wine is fine, but try to use white Bordeaux or a wine with subdued fruit, high acidity, and minimal oaking.*

**Serves 5**

**1** Pour 1 teaspoon of crème de cassis into the bottom of each wineglass, add 1 teaspoon of fresh lime juice, and top up with white wine.

**2** Place a sliver of lime peel on the top and serve.

**5 teaspoons crème de cassis (black-currant liqueur)**

**5 teaspoons lime juice**

**1 bottle dry white Bordeaux wine**
*well chilled*

**5 pieces lime peel**

Most of the people who contributed to this book would be unaware that they were playing such an important part in the sharing and celebration of traditional Vietnamese cuisine. Most of them will never see the book. They are the people who tirelessly cook and serve food on the street and still find the energy to chat to their customers; those who sell the best ingredients they can find, in markets up and down the country and make sure you get your share of them; those who enthusiastically guide visitors through restaurant menus and show them how to wrap, roll, and dip at the table.

Other people understood precisely the nature of my research, and those I can personally thank for their help and support. In Nha Trang, I would like to thank my great friend Aline Ho; also Nguyen Anh Son, Dang Ngoc Lai, and everyone at Ana Mandara who ensured I was out and about at dawn and dusk to observe the street eating.

Albert Claeys at the Furama Danang gave me access to his kitchen at all hours and even during service; within that kitchen particular thanks go to Phan Van Minh for painstakingly careful answers to questions.

In Hanoi, my thanks to Nguyen Thanh Van, Eric Simard, Sarah Grant, and everyone in the kitchen at the Hotel Sofitel; to Christina Yu for sending me off to the best *bun cha* shop ever.

In Ho Chi Minh City, first thanks must go to the amazingly knowledgeable Dieu Ho, and also to Nuoc Tinh who has the sweetest smile; to Thanh Thuy and her family who invited me to their home for a cooking lesson, and to Helen Lowy at the New World Hotel Saigon; to Quach Thien Tuong, Deena Hanley, and the management of the Omni Saigon Hotel for their on-going support; similarly thanks to Pierre Camorani at the Century Saigon Hotel. Grateful thanks to Alexander Egert at Camargue for the big picture. I cannot imagine someone more helpful than businesswoman Lu Khanh Anh—she and her sister are the most sophisticated home cooks I have met in Vietnam. Thanks also to gallery owner Do Huy Bac for restaurant recommendations and for introducing me to his coterie of wonderful friends, including Do Thi Tuyet Mai of Montana Restaurant.

In Hong Kong, many thanks to Mylinh Lee (and her mother To Ha Lee in Melbourne) and to the chefs and management of Vietnamese restaurants, Café au Lac and Indochine. And thanks to Carlos for tireless tasting.